THE WORD AND THE WAY OF THE CROSS

Christian Witness Among
Muslim and Buddhist People

by
Mark W. Thomsen

**DIVISION FOR GLOBAL MISSION
EVANGELICAL LUTHERAN CHURCH IN AMERICA
CHICAGO**

THE WORD AND THE WAY OF THE CROSS: CHRISTIAN WITNESS
AMONG MUSLIM AND BUDDHIST PEOPLE

Cover design: Michael Watson

Printed by Augsburg Fortress, Publishers

Printed in U.S.A.

DEDICATED

To all who witness to Jesus, the Cosmic Crucified.

CONTENTS

FOREWORD

At least for the past three decades, the discussion on the "pain" and the "suffering" of God has gone on with renewed intensity. More than 20 years ago it was first suggested that this notion of God's "vulnerability" was of crucial importance, especially for Christian-Muslim dialogue. In this study, Dr. Mark Thomsen places his reflections on "the continuing suffering-with-us God" in a double context (especially chapter 2, The Word of the Cross). In chapter one he articulates his conviction that as a Christian one can fully recognize the "footprints of God in all of history," including all cultures and religions, and yet maintain the affirmation that "Jesus the Cosmic Crucified" transcends all historical and cultural relativity. The third chapter, The Way of the Cross, gives the *human* context: discipleship is bound to be costly because of "God's call to vulnerability in mission."

In recent times many have stressed the experience of our human vulnerability as an aspect of interfaith *dialogue*. Thomsen's emphasis on vulnerability as an integral dimension of *mission* is one of the reasons why his study is so important, not only for those who continue to think of mission in (be it very subtle!) "imperialist" terms, but also for those who reject the idea of mission altogether as the expression of a most reprehensible arrogance. Thomsen's study (with four concluding chapters on "dialogue and witness among Buddhists and Muslims") is therefore a significant contribution to the far from closed debate on the issue of mission and/or dialogue.

Willem A. Bijlefeld
Director *Emeritus*
Duncan Black McDonald Center
Hartford Seminary

Hartford, Connecticut
April 1993

ACKNOWLEDGEMENTS

This study in Christian mission and witness is the result of years of biblical and theological discussion with family, friends, students, missionaries, and other colleagues. It would be impossible to recognize all of those who have contributed to the content of this volume; however, I do want to thank all of those who have voluntarily given hours of their time to work as members of a number of task forces which produced earlier mission documents which deeply influenced the present book.

The American Lutheran Church's Board for World Mission and Inter-Church Cooperation Task Force on Christian Witness Among Muslims (1984-1986) produced *God and Jesus: Theological Reflections for Christian-Muslim Dialog*, 1986:

Dr. Willem A. Bijlefeld
Dr. Carl E. Braaten
Dr. Terence E. Fretheim

Dr. Delvin D. Hutton
Dr. Robert W. Jenson
Dr. Paul Varo Martinson

The American Lutheran Church's Board for World Mission and Inter-Church Cooperation Task Force on Christian Witness Among Buddhists (1986-1988) produced *Suffering and Redemption: Exploring Christian Witness Within a Buddhist Context*, 1988:

Ms. Joyce Ditmanson
Dr. Terence C. Fretheim
Dr. Theodore C. Fritchel
Dr. Kosuke Koyama

Dr. Paul Varo Martinson
Dr. Merrill Morse
Dr. Paul R. Sponheim

The Evangelical Lutheran Church in America's Task Force on a Mission Statement (1989-1990) produced *Commitments for Mission in the 1990s*:

Dr. Carl E. Braaten
Dr. Terence C. Fretheim
Ms. Bonnie L. Jensen

Dr. William E. Lesher
The Rev. Barbara K. Lundblad
Dr. Winston D. Persaud

I also want to thank those who read the final drafts of *The Word and the Way of the Cross* and responded with critical suggestions: Dr. Willem A. Bijlefeld, Dr. James H. Burtness, The Rev. Michael G. Fonner, Dr. Terence C. Fretheim, Dr. Yoshiro Ishida, Ms. Bonnie L. Jensen, Dr. Paul Varo Martinson, Dr. Roland E. Miller, the Rev. Duane A. Olson, Dr. Edmund F. Perry, Dr. Duane A. Priebe and Dr. Paul R. Sponheim.

I want to thank my wife, Mary Lou. For forty years we have shared a mission adventure. While in Africa in the 1950s and 60s, she typed and edited earlier lectures and papers which became the foundation for *The Word and the Way of the Cross*. Finally, I wish to thank Ms. Karen Schneewind, who over the last ten years with meticulous skill has typed and edited innumerable drafts of all of the mentioned documents.

Mark W. Thomsen
Executive Director
Division for Global Mission
Evangelical Lutheran Church in America

Chicago, Illinois
April 1993

PREFACE

The board of the Division for Global Mission at its October 1990 meeting adopted a missiological document consisting of nine commitments, entitled *Commitments for Mission in the 1990s*. The nine commitments were subsumed under the basic mission statement, "The primary task of Christ's church is to proclaim Jesus Christ as Savior and Lord." The document was well received throughout the church.

The commitment document had been preceded by a background statement that focused on a missiology of the cross. This statement was primarily a response to the demand made by several theologians and missiologists who called Christian missionaries to stop affirming the finality of Christ. They state that one cannot declare the finality of Jesus Christ without becoming arrogant and imperialistic in mission. The primary thesis of the background statement was that because Jesus crucified had been raised, the nature of Jesus' lordship as suffering servant precluded arrogant imperialism and called for a form of mission molded by the self-giving service of Jesus Christ.

This basic motif in the background document became Commitment 5 in the brief commitments statement. This short missionary manual takes that focus on the cross of Jesus, the Cosmic Crucified, and shows how this basic motif addresses not only the missionary life-style, but how it has the capacity to mold the gospel message in ways that effectively and powerfully speak to Muslim and Buddhist peoples. These two religious communities are specifically addressed because the Division for Global Mission (DGM) through a board statement made witness among Muslims and Buddhists one of the major priorities for its future work.

This missionary manual was written for DGM's first seminar on Islam held for new missionaries preparing to work among Muslim peoples. The seminar was held at Carthage College, Kenosha, Wisconsin, July 26 to August 7, 1992. This statement also provides a rationale to members of the Evangelical Lutheran Church in America (ELCA) and other interested people as to why and how DGM intends to pursue its priority of witnessing among Muslim and Buddhist peoples.

COMMITMENTS FOR MISSION IN THE 1990s
Division for Global Mission
Evangelical Lutheran Church in America

*"But you will receive power when the
Holy Spirit has come upon you; and you
will be my witnesses . . . to the ends
of the earth" (Acts 1:8).*

The primary task of Christ's church is to proclaim Jesus Christ as Savior and Lord.

In order to proclaim Jesus Christ faithfully and globally, the Division for Global Mission of the Evangelical Lutheran Church in America makes the following commitments:

1. Background

Our world of five billion people is deeply marred by sin and its consequences. Humanity has turned away from God and insists on walking its own disastrous way. Contrary to God's vision for human life and creation, the world is permeated with enmity, greed, conflict, guilt and death and lies under the judgment of God. Broken and suffering, the world waits for its redemption.

The gospel announces that God in love sent Jesus Christ into the world as Savior to call for the world's repentance and to die for the sins of the world. Raised from death, Jesus Christ is God's victory over sin and death and is God's promise of a new creation.

There are two billion people who have not had the opportunity to hear this gospel. Another one and one-half billion persons have a minimal knowledge of Christ. There are, then, three and one-half billion persons who have not had the possibility of responding to God's saving gospel which promises justification by grace through faith in Jesus Christ and new life empowered by the Holy Spirit within the body of Christ; therefore:

Commitment

We are committed to proclaim to those who have not heard or who have not fully heard the gospel that Jesus Christ is Savior and Lord in order that they might believe.

2. Background

Christian congregations are centers of mission. The Holy Spirit through the ministry of Word and Sacrament calls, creates and nurtures ever-new communities of Christians. These persons, empowered by the Holy Spirit, are sent into the world to witness to Jesus Christ. In order that centers of Christian proclamation and witness may be multiplied:

Commitment

We are committed to the planting and growth of new congregations and churches where Christ is not yet known so that Christ might be more widely proclaimed and more fully known.

3. Background

In our religiously plural world, we have learned from people of other faiths that the great religious traditions offer life-sustaining power to their peoples. These religious communities challenge the validity of our witness among people of other faiths.

Many other people live their lives without claiming religious beliefs and/or values, some despairing of trust in God, some unable to relate scientific understanding to God's truth.

Within this pluralistic world, we believe and reaffirm: That God was incarnate in Jesus Christ; and that Jesus Christ was raised from the dead and sits at the right hand of God as Lord and Savior of all. Even though this incarnate God is unknown to people, the Triune God is already present and active in their lives and desires that the depths of God's saving love in Christ might be known by them. God calls us into mission in order that all persons may know that God incarnate in Jesus Christ has died for all; therefore:

Commitment

We are committed to witness to people of other faiths that Jesus Christ has died for them and, as Savior and Lord, is the normative and unsurpassable revelation of God.

4. Background

Christians around the world live in daily contact with peoples of other faiths. We believe that peoples of various faiths should enter into mutual conversations and interfaith dialogue. Conversations should seriously explore one another's differences as well as seek to understand the power, beauty and integrity found in each other's faith. We believe Christians are called to enter such conversations and dialogue not knowing where they will go, but sustained by the hope that, in the end, every tongue shall "confess that Jesus Christ is Lord to the glory of God the Father" (Phil. 2:11); therefore:

Commitment

We are committed to inter-faith conversations and dialogue and through these encounters we will seek to understand persons of other faiths; we will listen to what God has to say to us through these conversations and through them we will witness to the crucified and risen Christ.

5. Background

We recognize that at times our witness to Jesus Christ has been misheard and misunderstood. Because of our cultural ties and enculturation we have often created the impression that Jesus' Lordship is synonymous with cultural and political domination. In sharp contrast to this, we believe that God in Jesus took the form of a servant, shared human suffering, embodied God's compassion and prophetic struggle for righteousness, and was crucified. It is this crucified servant who sits at the right hand of God as Lord and Savior; therefore:

Commitment

We are committed to proclaim that the risen Lord, Jesus Christ, is the crucified, suffering servant; and

We are committed to take part in God's mission in a manner that is in harmony with Jesus' servanthood.

6. Background

As we reach out to those who have not heard the gospel, we recognize that approximately 80 percent of them live in oppression and poverty. In contrast, God wills fullness of life for all people and all creation. We believe that Christ calls us in these circumstances to enter into the suffering of their lives. Within that relationship God calls us to witness faithfully to the gospel in both word and deed; therefore:

Commitment

We are committed to witness to Jesus Christ in both word and deed. We will preach the gospel and in Jesus' name we will seek to alleviate suffering and empower the weak and advocate for righteousness, justice and peace. We will work with the entire global community for justice, peace and the renewal of all creation.

7. Background

The church of Christ has encircled the globe and is present on every continent. By the year 2000, 60 percent of the Christian world will be found in Latin America, Africa and Asia. The ELCA is one family of faith surrounded by a multitude of Christian communities who share with us our life and mission in Christ. We are called to enter into these relationships in new ways, receiving and sharing each other's gifts for the sake of God's mission; therefore:

Commitment

> *We are committed to cooperation and interdependency within the global Christian family. We will receive the witness of our global partners as they challenge us to faithfulness in mission. We recommit ourselves to send missionaries and resources in order to witness to Jesus Christ and support our partners who reach out in mission in Jesus' name.*

8. Background

The global Christian family includes a wide variety of persons with marvelous gifts and talents. We recognize that racial, sexist and social prejudices have limited the effectiveness of God's mission by excluding countless persons from full participation in life and mission together. Racial prejudice still divides the Christian community and excludes capable persons from involvement in mission. Women in some churches cannot vote, much less be admitted to positions of leadership or the ordained ministry. The mission of the body of Christ is so great that it requires the gifts and talents of every one of the baptized; therefore:

Commitment

> *We are committed to developing a global mission program in which persons of every ethnic background, both women and men, are called and empowered to participate fully in the mission of Jesus Christ.*

9. Background

The Evangelical Lutheran Church in America has innumerable resources. As one of the largest Lutheran churches in the world, with a membership of five million baptized, the ELCA has many gifted and committed persons willing to share their witness and talents around the globe. Located in one of the wealthiest and most powerful nations in the world, it has tremendous financial resources capable of supporting vital global outreach. Of the monies raised by local congregations in 1990, only two percent supports mission outside the U.S.A.; therefore:

Commitment

We are committed to increasing the concern and the involvement of every member and every congregation in Christ's mission to the world. We will expand our awareness, renew our prayer life and increase our support for the sake of God's mission.

We will in faithful obedience respond to Christ's Great Commission: "Go therefore and make disciples of all nations, baptizing them in the name of the Father and of the Son and of the Holy Spirit, and teaching them to obey everything that I have commanded you." We will faithfully respond to that word from the Lord of the church, trusting the promise "I am with you always, to the end of the earth" (Mt 28:19-20).

INTRODUCTION

Christian witness among Muslim and Buddhist peoples is one of the most crucial challenges encountered by Christians today. These two faith communities, like Christianity, have had the capacity to transcend cultural and ethnic boundaries, permeating the lives of people and nations around the globe. They also challenge the Christian faith in unique theological ways. Islam challenges the Christian assertions that God became human and God's Christ died on the cross. Islam asserts that these Christian affirmations compromise the transcendent nature of Allah. Theravada Buddhism's challenge goes even deeper when it denies the reality of God or the relevance of God for human salvation.

According to recent statistics compiled by David D. Barrett there are within the global human family 5.48 billion people: 1.8 billion Christians, 968 million Muslims, and 330 million Buddhists.[1] Hindus number 720 million. However, Hinduism has not been able to sustain growth outside the boundaries of Indian culture. Islam and Buddhism represent strong, growing faith communities that "offer life-sustaining power to their peoples. These religious communities challenge the validity of our witness among peoples of other faiths."[2]

Christians within their engagement with Islam and Buddhism are forced to give an account of their faith. In doing so Christians are compelled to examine the truth and content of their own faith. What is it that Christians have to share with Muslims and Buddhists that constrains Christians to be present and witness in their midst? If the answer is simply Jesus Christ, how do we clarify and articulate our witness to the Good News we believe to have found in him? Furthermore, Christians know that their lives and cultures have often detracted from rather than enhanced their witness. How then do we approach Muslims and Buddhists in order that our witness through words and actions may not detract from our witness but authentically witness to Jesus crucified and risen?

---

[1]David B. Barrett, "Annual Statistical Table on Global Mission," *International Bulletin*, vol. 16, no. 1, January 1992, 26.

[2]*Commitments for Mission in the 1990s*," Division for Global Mission, Evangelical Lutheran Church in America, October 1990, No. 3.

In exploring Christian witness among Muslims and Buddhist peoples, the discussion will focus upon the centrality of Jesus. A focus upon Jesus as portrayed in the New Testament is essential to our discussion because Jesus is recognized as a person of gigantic proportions within the Muslim community and also of interest within the Buddhist community. Within Islam, Jesus is designated not only as one of the prophets sent to the children of Israel, but as a word from God (Surah 3:45); a sign and a mercy from God (Surah 19:21); one confirmed by the Holy Spirit (Surah 2:253); a witness on the day of judgment (Surah 4:159); and one like Adam in that he was created in Mary's womb (Surah 3:47). The Qur'an invites the Muslim community to be fascinated by Jesus. Buddhism, unlike Islam, predates Christianity by about 500 years. There seems to have been little or no contact between Buddhists and Christians until about two hundred years ago. Today, however, Jesus is often recognized by many Buddhists as a person of deep spiritual insight. Jesus' non-violent lifestyle is particularly attractive to Buddhist peoples. The Christian does not have to create an interest in Jesus; it is already present.

The focus of this statement will be upon Jesus, but particularly upon Jesus crucified. It is Jesus crucified who is Lord. The early apostles proclaimed that the one with nail-pierced hands was raised from the dead, sits at the right hand of God as Cosmic Lord and Savior. The kingdom/reign of God had come near and was present in the prophet of the kingdom who had been put to death in Jerusalem. God had been seen, heard and touched in the Lamb of God who had died for the sins of the world. The resurrection proclaimed that the future belonged to this Cosmic Crucified through whom God brings life from death.

In a multiplicity of ways the New Testament faith claims that Jesus crucified and risen has saving significance for the whole world and the totality of creation. God in the crucified Jesus became ultimately significant for all time, in all places and for all people. I have used the phrase Cosmic Crucified to designate this affirmation of faith.

It is the thesis of this document that a focus upon the costly, suffering love of God incarnate in the Cosmic Crucified (a theology of the cross) is the most effective and powerful way to articulate the gospel among Muslim and Buddhist communities today. A theology of the cross addresses a number of specific and significant issues that relate directly to witness among these religious communities.

First, within the world of Islam and Buddhism, the cross speaks effectively and powerfully of God in Jesus Christ, who calls and challenges Christians as disciples to take up their own crosses and follow the Cosmic Crucified. Christians as disciples are called to proclaim the gospel of this self-giving, vulnerable One. That is the *Word of the Cross*. They are also called to follow this Jesus into the pain of human existence; to participate in the humble, self-giving vulnerable love of the mission of this Christ who incarnates the coming of God's kingdom. That is the *Way of the Cross*. In contrast to all forms of Christian arrogance, intolerance and imperialism, Jesus' disciples are called to be servants washing people's feet, "Christ-minded" persons molded by the cosmic crucified: "Let the same mind be in you that was in Christ Jesus . . ." (Phil 2:5-11).

Second, within Islam, a theology of Jesus crucified speaks powerfully and effectively of the costly love of the suffering God who becomes vulnerable in the incarnation in order to assume responsibility for humanity's salvation through Christ's death on the cross. This is in striking contrast to Islam's focus on transcendence, power and invulnerability. Jesus, crucified outside the walls of the holy city Jerusalem, contrasts strikingly to the statesman-prophet Muhammad, who rode before an army into the holy city Mecca.

Third, within the Buddhist context, Jesus as the Cosmic Crucified speaks powerfully and effectively of costly love--the willingness of God to share suffering and brokenness (suffering or "unsatisfactoriness" is a basic Buddhist motif) in order to transform life marked by suffering and brokenness (rather than seek release from suffering as in Buddhism). Buddhists who live without trust in God as the source of salvation need and have a right to hear this new and different gospel.

Finally, a vast number of Muslim and Buddhist people live in societies permeated by poverty and oppression. A theology of the cross speaks effectively and powerfully of the compassion and suffering of the Cosmic Crucified, who continues to hear the cries of poverty-ridden, suffering people, including Muslim and Buddhist people. Jesus' prophetic message of God's demand for justice still must be heard among the world's poor and oppressed. Muslims and Buddhists must hear God's good news for the poor, God's demand for mercy, compassion and justice for them. They must hear of the crucified prophet who called for righteousness, and they must witness his seeming unanswered cry from the cross. They must hear of God's Easter answer as the crucified is raised from the dead.

This document's basic thesis, namely, that the gospel of the Cosmic Crucified is the most effective and powerful way to live and articulate the gospel among Muslims and Buddhists today, will be presented as follows.

Chapter 1, "Transcending Historical and Cultural Relativity: Jesus the Cosmic Crucified," responds to two critical charges addressed to Christian missionaries who believe they are called to be witnesses to Jesus Christ among peoples of other faiths. One charge states that it is impossible in a world of many faiths to claim that one manifestation of God is more true than another (historical and cultural relativism). The second charge is that one cannot claim finality for a particular revelation of God without becoming arrogant, intolerant and imperialistic. These charges are answered by asserting that it is precisely the crucified Jesus who is risen Lord.

The chapter begins by simply stating that the apostolic faith declares that Jesus crucified is raised from the dead, sits at the right hand of God and therefore transcends historical relativity. Christian witness and mission is rooted in that resurrection faith. At the same time the chapter argues that the finality of the Cosmic Crucified does not preclude God's presence and revelation in all history, cultures and religions. One can see the footprints of God in all of history while at the same time seeing through the biblical witness the face of God in Jesus Christ (2 Cor 4:6). Recognition of this fact is the first step in treating persons of other faiths with respect and dignity, rather than as the demonic enemy or those believing in religious nonsense. The chapter then argues that it is precisely in affirming the finality of Jesus crucified that one rejects arrogance, intolerance and imperialism in mission among Muslim and Buddhist people. The content of the chapter is presented in dialogue with two contemporary missiological antagonists, Carl Braaten and Wesley Ariarajah.

The chapter concludes with the conviction that the mission of the body of Christ, both its message and life-style, must be molded by a missiology of the cross.

Chapter 2, "The Word of the Cross: Jesus the Cosmic Crucified," briefly presents three dimensions of the meaning of Jesus' death. The chapter begins by noting that missiology can be approached in a variety of ways, but that a missiology of the cross has deep roots in Scripture and in the Lutheran tradition. This gives theological legitimacy to an effort that seeks to show that a missiology of the cross ("a focus upon the costly suffering love of God incarnate in the Cosmic Crucified") is the most powerful way to articulate and live the gospel among Muslims and Buddhists today.

Three different dimensions of meaning are seen in the death of the Cosmic Crucified. They are undeniable if the resurrection and the biblical faith are affirmed.

1. The cross of Christ is God's vulnerability unto death for the ungodly.
2. The cross of Christ is a culminating revelation of God's continuing passionate involvement in human brokenness and suffering.
3. The cross of Christ is God's struggle against the powers of darkness.

Each of these dimensions is explored with discussions of the particular relevance of each dimension for the missionary *message* of the body of Christ among peoples of other faiths, particularly Muslims and Buddhists. This chapter focuses upon the content of the message of the gospel proclamation.

Chapter 3, "The Way of the Cross: The Cosmic Crucified and Costly Missionary Discipleship," explores the significance of the Cosmic Crucified, a missiology of the cross, for the life-style of the bearer of the gospel who proclaims the lordship of the crucified Jesus. The chapter begins by describing Christian discipleship in mission as being conformed to the Cosmic Crucified. Both the New Testament and the Lutheran tradition are used to show the legitimacy, relevance and power of a missionary form of life that is conformed to Christ.

Then the chapter explores discipleship as conformity with God incarnate in Christ in the light of the three dimensions of the cross of Christ described in the previous chapter. This missiology of the cross makes it impossible for the Christian community to separate the mission message from mission deeds. The question is not debatable, as it was in Jesus' message and in his life.

1. Discipleship in mission as God's call to passionate involvement in human brokenness and suffering (the second dimension noted in chapter 2).
2. Discipleship in mission as God's call to participate in the messianic struggle for life in the midst of death. A theology of the cross is sometimes critiqued for appearing to accept or affirm the suffering of the poor and marginalized, thus contributing to their oppression. This missiology of the cross intentionally affirms the messianic struggle for mercy, righteousness, justice and peace (shalom) in order that the oppressed and crushed might experience liberation from the powers of evil and death (the third dimension noted in chapter 2).
3. Discipleship as God's call to vulnerability in mission (the first dimension noted in chapter 2).

Chapter 4, "Dialogue and Witness Among Buddhists and Muslims," briefly summarizes implications of the previous chapters for dialogue and witness among Muslims and Buddhists.

Chapter 5, "The Unique Theological Task of Engaging with Muslim Peoples in Dialogue and Witness," explores four major theological issues that continually reappear as Christians engage with Muslims around the globe.

Chapter 6, "The Unique Theological Task of Engaging with Buddhist Peoples in Dialogue and Witness," outlines six major discussions that continually challenge Christians and Buddhists as they witness to each other.

Chapter 7, "Implementing Mission Among Muslims and Buddhists," describes five dimensions of the mission task as Christians witness among Muslim and Buddhist peoples.

The conclusion centers in Jesus' words of declaration: "But you will receive power when the Holy Spirit has come upon you; and you will be my witnesses . . . to the ends of the earth" (Acts 1:8).

1
TRANSCENDING HISTORICAL AND CULTURAL RELATIVITY: JESUS THE COSMIC CRUCIFIED

A. The Challenge of Theological Relativism to Mission

Carl Braaten, in his volume, *No Other Gospel*, fears that recent theological developments that relativize the gospel threaten the very existence of the church and its mission.[3] "Christian theology is today teetering on the brink of suicidal confusion."[4] In contrast, Braaten reaffirms a biblical faith in the finality of Jesus Christ and of the appropriateness of the term "absolute" when applied to the eschatalogical kingdom of God proclaimed and revealed in Jesus.[5] Christianity itself and authentic apostolic mission cease to exist if and when the eschatological finality of Jesus Christ is questioned and denied.[6]

Why is Braaten so deeply concerned? What is the threatening Trojan Horse in our midst? Braaten sees the primary threat articulated clearly in the British theologian John Hick. "Today John Hick is carrying [the] relativistic interpretation of Christianity to an extreme, with uncompromising consistency."[7] John Hick advocates a Copernican revolution in theology, a switch from a traditional Christ-centered (Christocentric) theology to universalistic God-centered (theocentric) theology of religion. Hick argues that our experience of religious pluralism indicates that Jews, Christians, Muslims, Sikhs and Hindus worship an ultimate Being designated by them as Adonai, or God, Allah, Param Atma,

---

[3]Carl Braaten, *No Other Gospel: Christianity Among the World's Religions* (Minneapolis: Fortress Press, 1992) (hereafter cited as *No Other Gospel*).

[4]Braaten, *No Other Gospel*, 2.

[5]Braaten, *No Other Gospel*, 47.

[6]Braaten, *No Other Gospel*, 11.

[7]Braaten, *No Other Gospel*, 38.

Rama, or Krishna. Hick asks, "Do these names designate different gods or are these names for the same ultimate Being?" He suggests three possible answers: 1) there are many gods; 2) one faith-community worships God while the others vainly worship images existing in their imagination; and 3) the most probable is

> that there is one God, who is maker and Lord of all; that in his infinite fullness and richness of being he exceeds all our human attempts to grasp him in thought; and that the devout in the various great world religions are in fact worshipping that one God, but through different, overlapping concepts or mental images of him.[8]

Hick also argues that the Christian doctrine of the incarnation, with its claims to universal finality for Jesus Christ, is an early Christian myth that is no longer tenable in the 20th century.[9] Hick does affirm that Jesus has become for Christians our "sufficient and saving point of contact with God" and therefore there is something absolute about him for our experience, which justifies for us the absolute language which Christianity has developed. If we understand our confession in this way, "We can revere Christ as the one through whom we have found salvation, without having to deny other points of reported saving contact between God and man."[10]

Hick concludes we are picturing a future in which the different religious traditions no longer see themselves as rivals but as mutually enriching communities of faith who have various saving points of contact with God.

Paul Knitter, in his influential work, *No Other Name?*, concludes his volume with this vision of mutually enriching communities of faith (Knitter designates this approach as "unitive pluralism"):

> Whether Jesus does or does not prove to be final and normative, is not, really the central issue or the primary purpose of dialogue. The task at hand, demanded of Christianity and all religions by both the religious and the socio-political world in which they live, is that

---

[8]John Hick, "Whatever Path Men Choose is Mine," in *Christianity and Other Religions: Selected Readings*, eds. John Hick and Brian Hebblethwaite (Philadelphia: Fortress Press, 1981), 177-78.

[9]Hick, "Whatever Path Men Choose is Mine," 186.

[10]Hick, "Whatever Path Men Choose is Mine," 186.

the religions speak and listen to each other, that they grow with and from each other, that they combine efforts for the welfare, the salvation, of humanity.[11]

It is this relativistic approach to the world of religious pluralism articulated so consistently by John Hick and Paul Knitter that Braaten sees as a denial of apostolic faith and as undermining the biblical understanding of the apostolic imperative for mission. In an earlier book, Braaten wrote, "All we know is that we must witness to the truth of Christ in the midst of the world religions, or our faith is dead."[12]

The DGM *Commitments for Mission in the 1990s*" statement clearly asserts that within this theological discussion, it identifies with a missiological community which shares those convictions articulated by Braaten. It does not reflect the relativistic position represented by Hick and Knitter, but rather sees relativism transcended in the finality of Jesus the Cosmic Crucified. "We are committed to witness to people of other faiths that Jesus Christ has died for them and, as Savior and Lord, is the normative and unsurpassable revelation of God," reads Commitment 3. The finality of the Cosmic Crucified is rooted in Jesus' resurrection from the dead. He is risen and sits at the right hand of God.

Having clearly stated this article of faith, the DGM *Commitments* statement also strongly affirms the universal presence, activity and revelation of God (Commitments 3, 4 and 5), a major emphasis in Braaten's book, *No Other Gospel* in which chapter 4 is entitled "Christ Is God's Final, Not the Only, Revelation."[13] The question then remains, how does one relate the "exclusive" claims made of Jesus Christ to the "inclusive" affirmations of the presence, activity and revelation of God experienced by religious persons of many faiths?

B. Relativism's Accusation of Missionary Arrogance

One of the most articulate advocates of a theological relativism is Wesley Ariarajah, an ordained Methodist minister from Sri Lanka and Director of the Sub-Unit on Dialogue of the World Council of Churches. In his recent

---

[11]Paul F. Knitter, *No Other Name: A Critical Survey of Christian Attitude Toward the World Religions* (Maryknoll, New York: Orbis, 1985), 231 (hereafter cited as *No Other Name*).

[12]Carl Braaten, *The Apostolic Imperative* (Minneapolis: Augsburg Publishing House, 1985), 14.

[13]Braaten, *No Other Gospel*, 65ff.

publication, *Hindus and Christians: A Century of Protestant Ecumenical Thought*[14] (an excellent work based upon his doctoral dissertation), Ariarajah even points to the Christian bias of Paul Knitter when Knitter questions whether "Jesus of Nazareth will stand forth (without being imposed) as the unifying symbol, the universally fulfilling and normative expression of what God intends for all history."[15]   What makes Ariarajah's discussion extremely significant is the fact that he is an Asian Christian who has always lived and reflected on his Christian faith and ministry within an Asian and primarily a Hindu context.

Carl Braaten's debate is primarily within a theological community in which secular and relativistic value systems have permeated our culture. Christian theologians academically discuss the finality of Christ. Ariarajah's concern arises out of an Asian pastoral ministry in which Christian claims to the finality of Christ often led to ministries and witness that were marked by arrogance and intolerance rather than what Kosuke Koyama calls the "crucified mind" of Christ.[16] This experience compels Ariarajah to continually note that Christian affirmations concerning the finality of Jesus Christ have of seeming necessity led to Christian arrogance and intolerance. In the closing chapter of *Hindus and Christians*, he asserts: "Our study of developments within the [Asian] ecumenical movement has shown that every attempt to reflect theologically about other faiths that has begun with the finality of Jesus Christ, interpreted in its various forms, has ended in Christian chauvinism and paternalism."[17] He concludes that the terms "finality and uniqueness" are obsolete because of the inherent negative implications for Christian relationships and witness among peoples of other faiths.

This conclusion, however, has not led Ariarajah to conclude with Braaten that "Christian theology is today teetering on the brink of suicidal confusion." It rather has driven him back to the biblical tradition to attempt to discover another approach to religious pluralism. In an earlier publication he wrote: "I am firmly convinced that there is in the Bible

---

[14]Wesley Ariarajah, *Hindus and Christians: A Century of Protestant Ecumenical Thought* (Grand Rapids: Eerdmans Publishing, 1991) (hereafter cited as *Hindus and Christians*).

[15]Ariarajah, *Hindus and Christians*, 206, quoting from Knitters, *No Other Name*, 231.

[16]Kosuke Koyama, *Waterbuffalo Theology* (Maryknoll, New York: Orbis, 1974), 209ff.

[17]Ariarajah, *Hindus and Christians*, 211.

another attitude to people of other faiths that Christians in Asia and elsewhere need to recover and celebrate."[18]   Ariarajah then lifts up throughout the Bible themes that point to an inclusive rather than exclusive interpretation of the gospel and a path that leads to dialogue rather than confrontation.

Ariarajah begins with the biblical understanding of creation. One God is the creator of everyone, and there is no other provider but this one God. He writes: "People [who are themselves created in the image of God] may or may not have an adequate understanding of who this God is, and their worship may or may not do justice to their understanding of God; but ultimately they are all provided for by this one God. Therefore, from God's side there can only be one family, the human family."[19]

The universal creation theme is followed by universal human alienation from God (the fall) resulting in the universal judgment of the flood. However, it does not stop here, because the Bible goes "on to develop the concept of God's covenant relationship with the whole human family."[20]   The universal covenant made with Noah includes more than humanity, because a compassionate God embraces all living things.

The Bible places the story of the chosen Israel in this universal context and sees the election of Israel as a means whereby God will bless all nations through Israel. "I will give you as a light to the nations, that my salvation may reach to the end of the earth" (Is 49:6b). The early Christian community saw this prophetic vision being fulfilled in Jesus Christ and the mission of the body of Christ. "But you are a chosen race, a royal priesthood, a holy nation, God's own people, in order that you may proclaim the mighty acts of him who called you out of darkness into his marvelous light" (1 Pt 2:9). Ariarajah points out that as a consequence of this biblical history, there are two communities of faith (Judaism and Christianity) who identify themselves as instruments of God's light. May it not be possible, argues Ariarajah, that God may also have called and chosen other nations whose divine election lies outside of the scope of the biblical narrative?[21]

---

[18]Wesley Ariarajah, *The Bible and People of Other Faiths* (Geneva: World Council of Churches, 1985), xiv.

[19]Ariarajah, *The Bible and People of Other Faiths*, 2.

[20]Ariarajah, *The Bible and People of Other Faiths*, 3.

[21]Ariarajah, *The Bible and People of Other Faiths*, 5ff.

Ariarajah states that the Bible itself may give glimpses of a universal activity of God who in love chooses, calls and judges all nations. Amos, chapters 1 and 2, declares God's particular judgment upon a cluster of Middle East kingdoms, including Damascus, Edom, Moab, Gaza, Tyre, Ammon, as well as Judah and Israel. The Lord roars from Zion because the kingdom of Moab burned to lime the bones of the king of Edom (Amos 2:1). The Lord is passionately concerned about the conduct and the fate of people beyond the covenant with Israel and Judah. Ariarajah states that the prophet goes even further in saying that God has been in the history of these nations because, "'I brought the Philistines from Crete and the Syrians from Kir, just as I brought you [Israel] from Egypt'" (Amos 9:7).[22] God is Lord of history and the nations. This is most powerfully announced in Isaiah 45 when Cyrus, king of Persia, is designated as the Lord's chosen. The Lord has chosen Cyrus to be king. He has appointed him to conquer nations (Is 45:1). A peculiar passage in Isaiah 19 brings to an eschatological climax this prophetic vision of God's relationship to the nations:

> On that day there will be a highway from Egypt to Assyria, and the Assyrians will come into Egypt, and the Egyptians into Assyria, and the Egyptians will worship with the Assyrians. On that day Israel will be the third with Egypt and Assyria, a blessing in the midst of the earth. (Is 19:23-24)

Ariarajah notes that Israel's own prophets insist that the God who called Israel out of Egypt cannot be locked up as Israel's private property. Christian theology, like this biblical tradition, "should allow God to be God."[23]

It is fascinating to read Genesis 21:8ff within the context of Christian-Muslim conversations. When Hagar and Ishmael are sent out from the house of Abraham and as they are at the point of dying in the wilderness, God speaks to Hagar:

> "What troubles you, Hagar? Do not be afraid; for God has heard the voice of the boy where he is. Come, lift up the boy and hold him fast with your hand, for I will make a great nation of him." (Gn 21:17b-18)

---

[22]Ariarajah, *The Bible and People of Other Faiths*, 7.

[23]Ariarajah, *The Bible and People of Other Faiths*, 11.

Ariarajah also sees the Jesus of the Synoptics reflecting this inclusive prophetic theme. Jesus announces the coming reign of God. "Jesus' own life is entirely God-centered, God-dependent and God-ward."[24] Ariarajah could also have noted, but did not, that in Luke, Jesus infuriated his own neighbors, the people of Nazareth, by pointing to the inclusivity of God:

> "But the truth is, there were many widows in Israel in the time of Elijah, when the heaven was shut up three years and six months, and there was a severe famine over all the land; yet Elijah was sent to none of them except to a widow at Zarephath in Sidon. There were also many lepers in Israel in the time of the prophet Elisha, and none of them was cleansed except Naaman the Syrian." When they heard this, all in the synagogue were filled with rage. (Lk 4:25-28)

Ariarajah's search for the inclusive tradition in Scripture concludes with two encounters: Jonah's call to preach repentance to Nineveh, and Peter's call to preach the gospel to the gentile Cornelius.[25]

In both situations, God had to overcome the exclusive parochial vision of God's spokespersons in order that the inclusive vision of God might be fulfilled. In Jonah's case, God's mercy was extended even to the foreign military terrorists of the seventh century B.C. Angry and disgusted with God's grace, Jonah resented God's forgiveness of the repentant Ninevites only to hear:

> "And should I not be concerned about Nineveh, that great city, in which there are more than a hundred and twenty thousand persons who do not know their right hand from their left, and also many animals?" (Jon 4:11)

In Peter's case, God, through a vision, told a reluctant Peter that God has not created anything clean nor unclean (profane nor sacred), whether it be animals or humanity. Peter's vision of exclusivity is transformed by a divine vision of inclusivity: "I truly understand that God shows no partiality, but in every nation anyone who fears him and does what is right is acceptable to him" (Acts 10:34).

---

[24]Ariarajah, *The Bible and People of Other Faiths*, 21.

[25]Ariarajah, *The Bible and People of Other Faiths*, 13-18.

Ariarajah in a sense pleads with the Christian community to take note of this often hidden or lost theme that runs through the biblical tradition. From his perspective, it is only by tapping this tradition that Christians can be prevented from encountering peoples of other faiths in arrogance and intolerance. Ariarajah, himself, says that this was his own experience. "It was while preparing for a Bible study on the book of Jonah that I 'saw' the radical nature of its message. My interest in dialogue was kindled, and I came to a new awareness of the theological significance of my neighbors of other faith convictions. For me the Bible has never been the same again!"[26]

It needs to be noted that many Christian theologians have explored and affirmed this inclusive theme within the Bible without negating the exclusive understanding of Jesus Christ, as is done by Ariarajah. Braaten recognizes, in the words of a chapter title, that "Christ Is God's Final, Not the Only, Revelation." Protestant theologians like Paul Althaus (Lutheran), Emil Brunner (Reformed), Paul Tillich (Lutheran) and Wolfhart Pannenberg (Lutheran); Catholic theologians like Karl Rahner and Hans Küng; the Asian theologians Raimundo Pannikar (Catholic) and Stanley J. Samartha (Protestant), and many others have affirmed this inclusive theme while at the same time affirming Jesus Christ's unique role.[27] Braaten, for example, interprets this universal dimension of the faith from an eschatological perspective. The risen Jesus Christ is "the personal event in whom God's final revelation has already occurred."[28] God, however, is at work in other communities of faith. The gospel announces that Jesus Christ is the goal to which God has been leading them all along. "The gospel declares that Christ is the manifestation of the truth of what all things shall become in their fullness."[29] Jesus Christ is universal, the church is not. "The church humbly shows to the other religions that it is also on the way,"[30] and the full meaning of Christ is explored and articulated as new peoples of new cultures and religions interpret Jesus Christ from their ever new perspectives.

---

[26]Ariarajah, *The Bible and People of Other Faiths*, 13.

[27]For excellent surveys of these views, see Paul Knitter's *No Other Name?* and Wesley Ariarajah's *Hindus and Christians*.

[28]Braaten, *No Other Gospel*, 3.

[29]Braaten, *No Other Gospel*, 10.

[30]Braaten, *No Other Gospel*, 11; see also Braaten's *The Flaming Center: A Theology of Christian Mission* (Philadelphia: Fortress Press, 1977), 93-119 (hereafter cited as *The Flaming Center*).

The Division for Global Mission's Commitments for Mission in the 1990s" statement also affirms this inclusive-exclusive theme reflecting its Lutheran roots which, in trinitarian fashion, holds the biblical understanding of creation and salvation together.   In Pauline terms, we have affirmed ". . . it is the God who said, 'let light shine out of darkness,' who has shone in our hearts to give the light of the knowledge of the glory of God in the face of Jesus Christ" (2 Cor 4:6).   In Commitments 3 and 4, it is stated, "Even though this incarnate God is unknown to people, the Triune God is already present and active in their lives."   Because the Triune God is present, these religious traditions "offer life-sustaining power to their peoples" and the religious traditions manifest "power, beauty and integrity." This same Triune God, however, "desires that the depths of God's saving love in Christ might be known by them" (see Commitment 3).

C. Compromising the Exclusive "Biblical Tradition"

Knitter and Ariarajah, as advocates of a theological relativism or Copernican revolution in Christian theology (moving from a christocentric to a theocentric perspective), are thoroughly aware that the New Testament makes numerous exclusive claims concerning Jesus, the Christ.   Paul Knitter writes:

> There is another feature of New Testament christology that the previous section did not treat . . . much of what the New Testament says about Jesus is *exclusive*, or at least *normative*. Jesus is the "one mediator" between God and humanity (1 Tim. 2:5). There is "no other name" by which persons can be saved (Acts 4:12). Jesus is the "only begotten Son of God" (John 1:14). No one comes to the Father except through him (John 14:6). Just as all died in one man, Adam, so all will be brought to life in one man, Christ (1 Cor. 15:21-22). What took place in him was, once and for all (*epaphax*). (Heb. 9:12)[31]

Knitter states that this exclusive theme is undeniable. Therefore, the question is raised as to how these exclusive claims are to be interpreted when one has accepted theological relativism and the inclusive theocentric model as normative. Both Ariarajah and Knitter see an answer in

---

[31]Knitter, *No Other Name*, 182.

interpreting exclusive language as confessional language analogous to personal language rooted in relationship and commitment. Both Ariarajah and Knitter use analogies from the personal language of love. Ariarajah writes, "When my daughter tells me that I am the best daddy in the world, and there can be no other father like me, she is speaking the truth. For this comes out of her experience."[32]

Knitter, in a similar vein, asserts, "Exclusivist christological language is much like the language a husband would use of his wife (or vice versa): 'You are the most beautiful woman in the world' . . . Such statements in the context of the marital relationship and especially in intimate moments are true."[33]   In the realm of personal language, these statements are true; however, in another sense they are not necessarily objectively true statements. It is argued that the exclusive claims for Christ are faith/ confessional statements made by believers whose "love" experience with Christ leads to true, but not absolutely true, statements about their Lord.[34]

Ariarajah writes: "The problem begins when we take these confessions of personal experience and preference and turn them into absolute truths. It becomes much more serious when we turn them into truths on the basis of which we begin to measure the truth or otherwise of other faith-claims."[35] Ariarajah asserts that absolute claims are not possible from a fallible human perspective. Furthermore, when absolute claims of truth are made, intolerance, arrogance and unwarranted condemnation of others immediately arise. This does not mean that Christians will not or should not make their own personal faith statements concerning their personal or communal convictions and commitments arising from their encounter with God in Jesus Christ. However, such statements, concerning God are to be seen within the context of other faithful persons and faith communities who have looked for God's universal revelation through other windows of faith.

It is at this point that Ariarajah and Knitter are to be challenged. We will continue to insist that our personal faith language concerning Jesus Christ is not only language of personal preference, but we believe it is intended by God to be ultimately the personal faith language of all people and all nations. That conviction is grounded in Jesus' resurrection from the

[32]Ariarajah, *The Bible and People of Other Faiths*, 25.

[33]Knitter, *No Other Name*, 185.

[34]Knitter, *No Other Name*, 182.

[35]Ariarajah, *The Bible and People of Other Faiths*, 26.

dead. We believe that it is God who has raised Jesus and in so doing announces that historical relativity has been transcended in the Cosmic Crucified.

Having asserted the historical relativity of the gospel, Ariarajah then moves on to claim that dialogue, openness to people of other faiths, and mutual enrichment through shared life and conversations flow from the heart of the Bible, the good news concerning God's love, the nature of God's love, and what that love meant in terms of God's relationship to the world.

Christians speak of this love as a consequence of meeting God in Jesus' life and ministry. Christians "were convinced that, meeting [Jesus], they came into a living encounter with God"[36] and God, seen through Jesus, is a loving God who leads persons into relationships, into dialogue. Ararajah draws this conclusion from the nature of God's love revealed in Jesus' life and mission.

God's love revealed in Jesus is first of all unconditional and prevenient. Jesus' love extends to persons before any positive response is present. God makes the sun to shine and the rain to fall on evil as well as good people, on Jesus' mother's garden as well as the vineyards of Herod the King (Mt 5:45). Jesus ate and drank with outcasts and sinners before there were signs of repentance. Significantly, Jesus had time for children even when they were considered a waste of time for his disciples. Ariarajah writes:

> Here the biblical message is unambiguously dialogical. For it insists on the "previousness" of grace, and of God's acceptance of us before our acceptance of God. The people we meet, of whatever religion, race or age, are all in that sense people of God. It is this belief that the other person is as much a child of God as I am that should form the basis of our relationship with our neighbors. That attitude is at the heart of being in dialogue.[37]

Furthermore, Ariarajah states that dialogue is at the very heart of the cross; for the cross, if nothing else, stands for the vulnerability of love. God in Jesus would accept the rejection by humanity before rejecting humanity. God's love in Jesus' cross wills to be self-giving, available, vulnerable, prevenient and unconditional. The incarnation, in this sense, is

---

[36]Ariarajah, *The Bible and People of Other Faiths*, 31.

[37]Ariarajah, *The Bible and People of Other Faiths*, 32.

God's dialogue with the world; "it is an expression of how God always stands [in love] with the human community."[38] Christian mission in response to God's love revealed in Jesus will be molded by this love of God. Ariarajah writes:

> Religious pluralism, let me repeat, does not demand that people give up or hide the witness they have to offer. But it certainly demands that such witness is given in the spirit of one who has truly experienced the humility, the vulnerability and the self-giving that are at the center of Christ's own witness. Such a witness can only be given in the context of a larger vision of the mission of God in which we are partners and fellow pilgrims with all others who also stand within the grace and love of God.[39]

Ariarajah has powerfully argued that authentic Christian witness must be molded by the mind of Christ. He is deeply concerned about this, because he has experienced the devastating consequences created by Christian arrogance and intolerance among Asian peoples. It is this concern that is of primary importance for the Division for Global Mission/Evangelical Lutheran Church in America as it seeks to witness to Jesus Christ within the world of religious pluralism; however, we desire to affirm that concern without forfeiting, as Ariarajah has done, our conviction that Jesus crucified and risen is God's final revelation. We are convinced that our personal faith language is intended by God to be and ultimately will be the personal faith language of all humanity. "Every tongue will confess that Jesus is Lord" (Phil 2:11).

Ariarajah's concern is reiterated by many voices from around the globe. When Professor Kosuke Koyama met with the American Lutheran Church/Division for World Mission and Inter-Church Cooperation task force assigned to explore Christian witness among Buddhist peoples, he stated emphatically that Western Christians should not and could not address an engagement of Christians and Buddhists in Asia unless they first confessed that the stance of many countries, organizations, churches and missionaries in Asia had been a stance of arrogance, paternalism and oppressive control. In contrast, Koyama calls all Christian missionaries out from a crusading mind-set to a crucified mind, the mind of Jesus Christ (Phil 2:5-11).[40]

---

[38]Ariarajah, *The Bible and People of Other Faiths*, 32.

[39]Ariarajah, *The Bible and People of Other Faiths*, 70-71.

[40]Koyama, *Waterbuffalo Theology*, 209ff.

A few years ago, Dr. Harold Vogelaar and I had the privilege of talking with the director of the Muslim Mission to the World. In the midst of the conversation, the director said, "How can there be genuine engagement between Muslims and Christians while Christian nations systematically destroy our Palestinian brothers on the Gaza strip?" As a Muslim, he saw the betrayal of the Palestinian people after World War I, when political independence had been promised and denied, and after World War II, when the traditional homeland of the Palestinian people had been given to Jewish immigrants, as a breach of human trust that made Christian and Muslim relationships tenuous at best. Muslim peoples had been subjugated to the military and political terror of the arrogant and imperialistic West.

The question is raised from around the globe as to the possibility of separating a Western missionary witness to Jesus Christ crucified from the dominating global power of our Western nations. That question is a primary question for the Division for Global Mission/ELCA. In many discussions I have found that some representatives of the Western Christian church find it difficult to take this question seriously. That has not been true in conversations with Christian partners from Latin America, Africa and Asia.

D. Affirming Cosmic Finality with the Vulnerability of Cosmic Love: A Missiology of the Cross

Braaten has reaffirmed an "exclusive" biblical faith within a philosophical and theological conversation marked by cultural and epistemological relativism. Faithfulness to the apostolic imperative and our own Christian convictions have led us to that same conclusion. We, as a Division for Global Mission/ELCA, are committed "to witness to people of other faiths that Jesus Christ has died for them and, as Savior and Lord, is the normative and unsurpassable revelation of God" (Commitment 3). The usefulness of the word "finality" may be questioned by some because it may intimate that God's saving and revealing work ceases with Jesus. For others, it may imply Christian imperialism, which is specifically denied here. I have chosen to maintain the word to make clear that the thesis of this document affirms the normativeness and unsurpassability of what happens and is revealed in Jesus the Cosmic Crucified. Everything we say and do is grounded in our conviction that Jesus is raised from the dead and transcends historical relativity. God's self-identifying, self-characterizing, action happens in Jesus crucified and risen. Jesus the Cosmic Crucified becomes the normative and unsurpassable revelation of God.

Having said this, how do we address those who experience and who claim that this "exclusive" position inevitably leads .to Christian arrogance and intolerance, which leads to human suffering, alienation and oppression? How do we affirm with Dr. Ariarajah that this is contrary to the mission of Jesus and the revelation of God through Jesus marked by self-giving, humility, openness and vulnerability? How do we do that without giving up our convictions that Jesus Christ is not only cosmic truth but absolute and final cosmic truth?

The Christian community does that by affirming that the risen Christ is precisely the crucified Jesus. The one with nail-pierced hands sits at the right hand of God. In affirming that the crucified is the one who transcends historical relativity, one makes absolute the self-giving, serving, sacrificial vulnerability of Jesus the Cosmic Crucified. It is precisely in exploring the dimensions of Jesus as the crucified one that one discovers the shape of the gospel that has the power to speak authentically among Muslims and Buddhists. Furthermore, it is within this witness and these conversations that we are driven back to affirm the cosmic finality of Jesus because one finds something wondrously unique about the gospel. Nowhere else does one encounter God in costly love entering so deeply, fully and sacrificially into human existence on humanity's behalf On a cosmic scale nothing greater can be conceived than that. To those skeptical of the reality of that gospel one can reply that if it is not true, one would hope that it could be or would be true. That, in and of itself, is an invitation to follow Jesus–to come and see a crucified Jewish prophet who Christians believe is the risen Cosmic Lord!

Our witness among Muslims and Buddhists reaffirms and strengthens our conviction that our personal language of faith in the love of God in Jesus crucified and risen is intended by God to be the personal faith language of all people. Until they know and trust that personal faith language, they have not understood who truly is at the heart of the universe; they have not fully known God. The Cosmic Crucified is the one who is to be preached to the nations as Savior and Lord, and the Cosmic Crucified calls all Christians to participate in the self-giving, serving, sacrificial vulnerability of Jesus.[41]

This presentation intends to claim Jesus Christ for a Christian perspective that humbly is open to listening, loving, serving and cooperating with peoples of other faiths, while at the same time witnessing humbly, joyfully and confidently to Jesus Christ among them. Often, in the present

---

[41]Carl Braaten has a chapter in *The Apostolic Imperative* entitled "The Cross as the Criterion of Christianity," 16-32.

discussion, the necessity of humility, vulnerability, self-giving love, service, cooperation is advocated by Christians who willingly speak of God but seem reluctant to talk about Jesus. I believe that the primary reason for this is that witness to Jesus has often been accompanied by exclusivism, arrogance and intolerance. The name of Jesus has in a sense been desecrated by Christian arrogance and intolerance. The name of Jesus deserves better within the Christian community particularly at this time within our Lutheran community. It is hoped that this missiological statement will do precisely that.

These convictions concerning the finality of the Cosmic Crucified lie at the center of the Division for Global Mission's *Commitments for Mission in the 1990s* and is articulated in Commitment 5:

5.   Background

We recognize that at times our witness to Jesus Christ has been misheard and misunderstood. Because of our cultural ties and enculturation we have often created the impression that Jesus' Lordship is synonymous with cultural and political domination. In sharp contrast to this, we believe that God in Jesus took the form of a servant, shared human suffering, embodied God's compassion and prophetic struggle for righteousness, and was crucified. It is this crucified servant who sits at the right hand of God as Lord and Savior; therefore:

Commitment

We are committed to proclaim that the risen Lord, Jesus Christ, is the crucified, suffering servant; and

We are committed to take part in God's mission in a manner that is in harmony with Jesus' servanthood.

Now it is necessary to explore more fully the implications of this approach to the understanding of our mission.

2

THE WORD OF THE CROSS: THE COSMIC CRUCIFIED

A. Costly Love--Costly Discipleship

God's love is revealed and active in the crucifixion of Jesus the Cosmic Crucified. In this event, God declares that divine love is self-giving, suffering and sacrificial. God in love is vulnerable unto death in our midst; therefore, God's love is costly. "You know that you were ransomed from the futile ways inherited from your ancestors, not by perishable things like silver and gold, but with the precious blood of Christ" (1 Pt 1:18-19b).

It is essential in our time and for our task that the gospel message centered in God's costly love be found in Jesus' paradoxical lordship. The one who was exalted to the right hand of God and before whom every knee will bow is the one who emptied himself, took the form of a servant and became obedient even to death on the cross (Phil 2:5-11). The New Testament proclaims repeatedly that the Risen Son of the Living God is the one who, as suffering servant, went through death and hell for the world's sake. There is the awesome miracle that he who was rich became poor (2 Cor 8:9); that the Word of God became flesh and lived among us (Jn 1:14); that the Lord washed his disciples' feet (John 13); that the Christ hung in the darkness of Calvary and died for the sins of the world (Jn 1:29).

The incredible, awesome wonder of the gospel is that God, the Creator, Molder and Future of the universe, was and is among us as a humble, suffering servant who willingly dies for the world. God has been here but not as we expected. Power appeared in seeming weakness, in compassion, service and sacrificial death. God in love has been the vulnerable one in our midst. The gospel was and is costly.

It is absolutely essential that we proclaim a gospel shaped by the Cosmic Crucified rather than a message shaped by our cultural values and norms. It is essential that it is Jesus crucified, not ourselves, who defines God and the mission of God. The marks of divine love incarnate in Jesus the Cosmic Crucified are: not self-service but self-giving and sacrifice for others; not indifference and distance but compassion as suffering-with love; not domineering arrogance but humble servanthood; not power and invincibility but vulnerability. That is incredible costly love. Nail-pierced hands and a wounded side are permanent marks of the risen one (John 20). The Christ we preach did not and does not come. as over-powering king but as suffering servant who dies for the healing of the nations (Isaiah 42, 49, 53). In contrast to our cultural values and norms, the gospel message is cruciform. Salvation is rooted in the vulnerable, costly love of God.

Also of primary significance is the fact that the messengers proclaiming the gospel be understood as participants in the mission of God incarnate in Jesus crucified. Not only our message must be formed and informed by the cross, but our style and form of presence in the world must be formed by the cross. As we proclaim Jesus Christ and salvation in Jesus' name, we are called to walk with Jesus the way of the cross: "Take up your cross and follow me!" (Mk 8:31ff). Costly grace calls forth costly discipleship. The Asian scholar, Choan-Seng Song, addressing the same missiological issue, asserts that many within the missionary movement were not able to distinguish between the brutal political power of the West and the saving power of love's vulnerability incarnate in Jesus.

> How different is this God of the pompous church and militant missions from the God of the cross! The God we encounter in Jesus on the cross is powerless and helpless. In this vast and rich universe, God has nothing to support Jesus but the two cruel wooden beams representing pain, shame and suffering. But this is precisely the God who has power to save the world.[42]

The followers of Jesus have been grasped by a cruciform gospel, by incredible costly love. We have been called to a cruciform style of mission and ministry, costly discipleship. We proclaim the gospel and follow Jesus within the power and shape of the cross, the price of our salvation. Our words and life are molded by Jesus crucified, for it is the crucified Jesus who is given the name above every name. What are the implications of a theology of the cross for our proclamation and understanding of the gospel, and for our understanding of our discipleship? What are the consequences of being called to speak and act in his name?

---

[42]Choan-Seng Song, *Third Eye Theology: Theology in Formation in Asian Settings* (Maryknoll, New York: Orbis Books, 1979, revised edition), 181 (hereafter cited as *Third Eye Theology*).

B.   Some Reflections on Methodology

God's mission and missioning people have been viewed and understood from a variety of perspectives. The church's participation in the mission of God has been rooted in: the apostolic imperative, "Go and make disciples of all nations" (Mt 28:20);[43] the church's pentecostal empowerment;[44] the trinitarian creedal formulation;[45] the biblical understanding of the kingdom of God;[46] and others. Each of these studies begins from a particular viewpoint and attempts to explore the rich dimensions of the mission of God from that perspective.

This particular missiological exploration begins by focusing upon Jesus as the Cosmic Crucified and from that viewpoint attempts to articulate the implications of this approach for understanding the mission of God and God's missioning people. The decision to begin with the cross is not arbitrary. As noted earlier, a focus upon the Cosmic Crucified as the presence and action of the suffering God speaks powerfully today both to Christians witnessing among Muslims and Buddhists as well as to Muslims and Buddhists. Of greater weight is the biblical fact that the cross is central to the New Testament's understanding of the gospel.

The death of Jesus is central to the New Testament. Passion narratives receive major emphases in the Gospels. The epistles of the New Testament often explore the depths of the faith from the perspective of the crucified and risen Lord. The awe and wonder of the early church are expressed by Paul, "While we were still weak [sinners], at the right time Christ died for the ungodly" (Rom 5:6). Therefore, I decided to know nothing among you except Jesus Christ, and him crucified" (1 Cor 2:2).
It is obvious that if Jesus had been crucified and remained dead, the disciples would have continued to say, "But we had hoped that he was the one to redeem Israel"(Lk 24:21). The Resurrection, however, became an experienced fact. Jesus, the crucified, was seen, recognized and known as risen. The Apostolic witness centered in these words, "The Lord has risen indeed, and he has appeared to Simon!" (Lk 24:34); to Mary (Jn 20:1-18); to the 12, to 500, to James, to all the apostles, to Paul (1 Cor 15:1-8).

---

[43]Braaten, *The Apostolic Imperative.*

[44]Harry Boer, *Pentecost and Missions* (London: Lutherworth, 1961).

[45]Lesslie Newbigin, *Trinitarian Faith and Today's Mission* (Richmond: John Knox Press, 1963).

[46]Emilio Castro, *Freedom in Mission: The Perspective of the Kingdom of God* (Geneva: World Council of Churches, 1985).

God had raised him and Jesus was proclaimed as the Cosmic Crucified who now poured out the power of the Spirit upon his disciples. That was and is awesome joy. C. S. Song writes:

> Theology should be an ode of love. . . . Theology without the pain and agony of love is not theology. It is a make-believe monologue directed to no one but itself. Nor is theology without joy and exultation true theology. It is an endlessly dull discourse that puts to sleep not only the audience, but the speakers themselves. Such a theology has nothing to do with the God of the Christian Bible who creates the world and redeems it in passionate love.[47]

The Lutheran tradition which the Division for Global Mission/ELCA represents also has a unique concern for the theology of the cross. Lutheran theology contrasts "a theology of the cross" with "a theology of glory," affirming the first and denying the latter. This emphasis upon the cross is rooted in Martin Luther's Heidelberg Theses of 1518 and permeates his thinking.[48] In contrast to a theology of the cross focused on the crucified Christ, a theology of glory focuses upon the all-conquering Christ and triumphalistic church. In a "theology of glory" faith sees God at work in a continual series of divine and ecclesiastical victories and conquests within history and epitomized in the dominating power and authority of the church within established Christendom. Faith is understood to be created, strengthened and proven by signs of God's power.

In contrast, in a theology of the cross, Luther points to the suffering of the cross in Jesus' life and to the seeming defeats and suffering of God's saints within history and affirms that God is present and revealed in weakness, in suffering, in the cross. God is "hidden" in our midst, and faith trusts contrary to appearances. Faith is a miracle of the Holy Spirit that continually affirms "nevertheless, I believe." The "nevertheless" of faith is central to Luther's theology of the cross. In Luther's explanation to the Third Article of the Creed, he states: "I believe that by my own reason or

---

[47]Song, *Third Eye Theology*, 108.

[48]Walther von Loewenich, *Luther's Theology of the Cross* (Minneapolis: Augsburg Publishing House, 1976).

strength I cannot believe in Jesus Christ, my Lord, or come to him. But the Holy Spirit has called me through the gospel, enlightened me with his gifts, and sanctified and preserved me in the true faith."[49]

Luther's theology of the cross also calls Christians to become like their Master in all things. The Christian life is one of lowliness and forsakenness; weakness and despair are marks of discipleship; faith is always "nevertheless!" Furthermore, the way of the cross means dying to that which is contrary to Christ within our lives and outwardly confronting the enmity of the world. "The world's enmity is a sign of the genuineness of discipleship."[50]   The Christian life is a continual struggle with the sinful self and the sinful world and is evidence that disciples have taken up their cross to follow Christ.

A theology of the cross also emphasizes human sinfulness in that humanity nailed God's incarnate truth to the cross and continues to ignore, reject and desecrate that truth. The depth of humanity's sin is revealed in the crucifixion of the Cosmic Crucified. Sin is revealed as ultimate distrust and rejection of God's cosmic centrality, God's primacy, God's ultimacy. This move away from God is the root cause of humanity's alienation from God and one another and hence the cause of humanity's brokenness and suffering.

The cross on the one hand is humanity's rejection of the cosmic centrality of God; however, on the other hand, the resurrection announces that the cross is God's, not humanity's, ultimate word in the cosmos. The cross is that event in which God redeems sinful humanity by taking the power of sin into God's own being while continuing to reach out in grace to the whole human community and the whole universe. The cross accuses of sin and announces God's costly grace.

A theology of the cross needs to be reaffirmed as we move toward the beginning of twenty-first century. Luther spoke powerfully of a theology of the cross in relationship to the life and mission of the church in the sixteenth century. The power of the church and its hierarchy, the attempts to establish salvation as the consequence of self-righteousness or self-justification, were critiqued by a theology of the cross. In contrast to the theology of glory, Luther presented a theology of the cross that glorified God and God's justifying grace manifest in the crucified and suffering one.

---

[49]Small Catechism in *The Book of Concord*, ed. Theodore G. Tappert (Philadelphia: Fortress Press, 1959), 345.

[50]von Loewenich, *Luther's Theology of the Cross*, 122.

The theology of the cross called Christians to a miraculous faith that through the Spirit trusted in the foolishness of God's seeming weakness and obediently took up the cross to follow Jesus in humble discipleship.

In focusing on the Cosmic Crucified, it is possible to tap both our Lutheran theological roots and to explore the ramifications of a theology of the cross for our contemporary missiological task.

Finally, it is the hypothesis of this book that this focus on the cross of the Cosmic Crucified will enable the Christian community to address primary issues confronting the contemporary church, which seeks to be authentically in mission among Muslims and Buddhists.

In seeking to understand the meaning of the Cosmic Crucified, three primary dimensions of the cross are described. They are undeniable aspects of the cross, when it is assumed that the resurrection faith declares that Jesus crucified is raised by God and made the risen Crucified, the Cosmic Crucified. Those dimensions are:

> 1) The cross reveals that God, in saving the world, is willing to be ultimately vulnerable unto death for the ungodly. This is a primary dimension of what has been designated the atonement (Section C).

> 2) The cross is a culminating revelation of God's continuing passionate presence within human life marked by brokenness, pain and suffering. That is a dimension of the totality of the atonement (Section D).

> 3) The cross reveals God's struggle against the powers of sin and evil in the world. Jesus as God's prophetic spokesperson for the kingdom/reign of God is opposed and rejected by those empowered by the principalities and powers. That also is a dimension of the totality of the atonement (Section E).

From an historical and organically progressive point of view, it would probably be better to place the heart of the atonement thoughts last. It is only as God in Christ becomes incarnate (No. 2 above), and only when Jesus within the conflict is crucified (No. 3 above) that the ultimate atoning power of God is realized and revealed (No. 1 above). However, from the point of view of "awe and wonder" and what is crucial to it all, the discussion begins with the heart of the atonement; that is, God's vulnerability unto death.

C.   Jesus the Cosmic Crucified: Divine Vulnerability
Unto Death for the Ungodly

In Jesus as Cosmic Crucified, we know that God through costly love opens God's own being to pain and suffering; that is, to being wounded and vulnerable even unto death! In contrast to ancient Greek philosophical views which still influence our theology and in contrast to our culture's glorification of power and domination, the God of the Scriptures is totally involved in human brokenness and suffering as suffering servant. Christians believe that God wills to be open to suffering, to bear suffering in order to save humanity from their own self-destruction. Suffering is not imposed upon a helpless God; rather, God, the Source of cosmic power, wills to be vulnerable to death for the world's sake. The Bible proclaims that God suffers because of us and for our salvation.

A number of Old Testament biblical pictures prefigure this suffering God who became incarnate in Christ, suffered and died for our salvation. God who as father or mother teaches Israel to walk and embraces them in God's arms, weeps as they walk to their own destruction (Hos 11:l-9); God as a mother in birth pangs gives birth to a new creation (Is 42:14-16); God as husband agonizes with an unfaithful spouse who deserts her husband and family, but then God redeems her and restores her to the home (Hosea 1-3). This prophetic understanding of the suffering love of God is also portrayed in Jesus' parables of the forgiving father who agonizes and then rejoices at his son's return, the shepherd who was anxious and then rejoiced in finding a lost sheep, and the woman who had lost and then found coins (Luke 15). God loves us passionately enough to be moved by us, affected by us, even wounded and pained by us. God suffers, and God is open to being wounded (is vulnerable) because God wills to relate to life and loves people. It is this suffering God incarnate in Jesus who is the ground of humanity's redemption. Grace is costly grace!

I remember first reading Kazo Kitamori's book, *The Theology of the Pain of God*, as a seminary student in 1956.[51] Interpreting the Hosea 11:8 passage, "How can I give you up, O Ephraim!", Kitamori spoke of the pain of God. The pain of God is rooted in love that first flows to and encompasses God's people. However, this first love is faced with a people

---

[51]Kazo Kitamori, *The Theology of the Pain of God* (Richmond: John Knox Press, 1965), 119-121. For a recent and exceptional study of the suffering of God in the Old Testament, see Terence E. Fretheim's book *The Suffering of God: An Old Testament Perspective* (Philadelphia: Fortress Press, 1984), Chapter 7 for a discussion similar to Kitamori's. Fretheim has two contributions in "God and Jesus: Theological Reflections for Christian-Muslim Dialog" (Division for World Mission and Inter-Church Cooperation, The American Lutheran Church, 1986, Photocopied) which articulate his unique contribution to theology in this area of biblical study.

of Israel who ignore, reject and desecrate this first love through faithlessness and disobedience. Faithlessness and disobedience arouse wrath in God which is repulsed by sin and desires to purge life of that which is evil and destructive. God's love is pained by sin and evil; however, it refuses to reject or exclude the object of wrath. The love of God, in spite of the pain and in the pain, fully embraces sinful humanity. Love which accepts and forgives is rooted in the pain of God. One of Kitamori's key verses is Jeremiah 31:20:

> Is Ephraim my dear son? Is he the child I delight in? As often as I speak against him, I still remember him. Therefore I am deeply moved for him; I will surely have mercy on him, says the Lord.

Kitamori's insight into the internal suffering of God is helpful in discussions within the Muslim community. Muslims often question Christians as to why God cannot freely forgive sin without requiring the sacrificial death of Jesus. It is helpful to speak of that suffering as in part the internal suffering of God analogous to the internal suffering of parents who love wayward and rebellious children, agonizing over their willful self-destruction, seeking for their repentance and renewal, and joyously welcoming them home in spontaneous but costly forgiveness. It is this suffering love of parents that makes forgiveness possible. This makes it clear that the suffering leading to forgiveness is not external to forgiveness nor haphazardly related to forgiveness, but it is suffering love that makes forgiveness possible. If forgiveness is not grounded in suffering love or in justice, as some Muslims would argue, but in divine *fiat* and ungrounded freedom as argued by other Muslims, then one's future is in the hands of an unknown God who forgives or does not forgive capriciously.

The biblical faith, however, roots forgiveness in suffering love, but it does not limit divine suffering to the inner being of God. God's love breaks into history in the Cosmic Crucified in order to seek the wayward and rebellious who intentionally despise and reject the God in Christ who seeks them. The depths of God's pain, reflected in the Old Testament and Jesus' teachings is seen, heard and touched in Jesus' messianic mission. Here the pain-filled heart of God becomes incarnate in a mission that seeks to save the rebellious and culminates on Golgotha. At Jerusalem's gates Jesus weeps for the city that would reject him and then is hung in the darkness of Golgotha. Here we powerfully and ultimately encounter not only the vulnerability of God's love to those who despised him but God's vulnerability to death for them in his Son: that is suffering love as God's infinitely costly saving power (Romans 1:16-17).

God in Jesus Christ is God who through the power of love insistently and persistently seeks and then draws all persons to the foot of the cross (Jn 12:32). Jesus in passionate concern pleads even for those who hung him on Calvary. Jesus tongue-lashed them for their hypocrisy, but he wept for them in their refusal to accept truth and life (Lk 19:41). God's power in Jesus is the power to persevere in a pain-filled mission even unto death. It is the power to forgive in the presence of humanity's continual "no!" It is the power to embrace in pain-filled love those who have refused and despised the best God could offer as God sought them through his own Son.

The unity of God and Jesus Christ is proclaimed by the resurrection. Robert W. Jenson writes, "Only the resurrection of the dead will verify Yahweh's self-introduction as God."[52] This unity is the foundation for our faith. We proclaim that Jesus' cross is also God's cross. We are compelled to say that the cross is not only Jesus' missionary way but God's missionary way in the world. Not only is Jesus involved and wounded within history, but God is involved and vulnerable within history. It is not just Jesus who forgives while nails are driven into his hands. God also forgives those who nailed Jesus' hands to a wooden cross.

Particularly within Islam it is important to make clear that Jesus' mission was God's mission; that God was in Christ reconciling the world to himself (2 Cor 5:18). Some Muslims particularly note that a traditional doctrine of the atonement makes a distinction between the wrathful justice of God and the mercy of Jesus who dies for the sins of the world.

Instead of maintaining the unity of God in Jesus, the Christian community has often portrayed the crucifixion as a struggle between God and Jesus for the future of sinful humanity. Forgiveness has been portrayed as the consequence of the sacrifice of Jesus, the Son of God, to the justice-demanding God, who demanded a terrifying compensation for sin. Muslims have concluded that Christians are polytheists who worship two different realities—a God of wrath-filled justice and a compassionate Son of God, Jesus. Christian witness within the Muslim community must make it clear that the biblical faith does not view God and Jesus in this antagonistic relationship. Jesus' costly love is God's costly love. Jesus' suffering and pain are God's suffering and pain. The cross of Jesus can never be portrayed as a merciful Jesus appeasing and transforming a wrathful, justice-demanding God. It must always portray the suffering and

---

[52]Robert W. Jenson, *The Triune Identity* (Philadelphia: Fortress Press, 1982), 39.

grieving of God incarnate in Jesus. In Paul's words, God was in Christ reconciling the world to himself (2 Cor 5:18). "For God so loved the world that he gave his only Son" (Jn 3:16).

Faith asserts that it is here on this particular hill and in this particular prophet from Nazareth that God absorbed the fanatic and tragic rejection of God's very best, God's own final truth, the Father's own Son (Mk 12:1-12). God accepts into God's own being the costly pain and suffering inflicted on Jesus in order that God's love may encompass or embrace the whole of humanity and all creation. Reconciliation is infinitely costly. Atonement and grace have their roots in the grieving God who struggles to bring life into the midst of death and in the tragic life and crucifixion of Jesus.[53]

Jürgen Moltmann in *The Crucified God* writes insightfully concerning the atonement in a section entitled a "Trinitarian Theology of the Cross." Kitamori looks into the inner being of God and sees atonement in God's love overcoming God's own wrath in pain. The Cosmic Crucified incarnates that love in living and dying. Moltmann, in seeking to understand the atonement, plumbs the relation of the Trinitarian Father and Son and focuses upon "the abandonment of Jesus by his God and Father" [p 242].[54] "My God, my God why have you forsaken me?" is reported as the dying words of Jesus by the Gospels of Mark and Matthew (Mk 15:34; Mt 27:46). This theme of abandonment is expressed by the Apostle Paul in Romans 8:31: "He who did not withhold his own Son, but gave him up for all of us, will he not with him also give us everything else?" (see also 2 Cor 5:21; Gal 3:13). Jesus the Son suffers, dying in forsakenness, but, Moltmann insists, the Father who abandons him and delivers him up suffers the death of the Son in the infinite grief of love.[55] It is this unconditioned and boundless love proceeding from the grief of the Father and the dying of the Son that reaches forsaken people with new life.[56]

---

[53]See Kenneth Cragg, *The Call of the Minaret*, revised (Maryknoll, New York: Orbis, 1989), 272.

[54]Jürgen Moltmann, *The Crucified God: The Cross of Christ as the Foundation and Criticism of Christian Theology* (New York: Harper and Row, 1974), 235-249 (hereafter cited as *The Crucified God*). For another interpretation of the atonement grounded in the unity of God and Jesus, see *The Essence of Christianity* by Anders Nygren (Philadelphia: Muhlenberg Press, 1961), 126-128. Nygren grounds atonement in God's willingness to pour out costly love upon selfish humanity even though it is spurned and trampled upon. This love designated "lost love" is the atonement.

[55]Moltmann, *The Crucified God*, 243.

[56]Moltmann, *The Crucified God*, 245.

For Moltmann, God is confronted by a world of lovelessness and law that abandons those who are unloved, forsaken and unrighteous outside the law. God wills life for this broken human community; however, God wills authentic life with freedom. Life apart from freedom is not human life; therefore, God cannot simply suppress lovelessness, enmity and slavery. The forceful suppression of lovelessness and enmity would destroy human freedom, which would destroy authentic human life. Therefore, if life is to be given, God must suffer the contradiction between humanity bound in "lovelessness and law" and humanity intended for life.

> [Divine love] can only take upon itself grief at this contradiction and the grief of protest against it, and manifest this grief in protest. That is what happened on the cross of Christ. God is unconditional love, because he takes on himself grief at the contradiction in men and does not angrily suppress this contradiction . . . *[Instead of suppressing humanity marked by lovelessness and law,] God allows himself to be crucified and is crucified, [in Jesus as Son] and in this consummates his unconditional love that is so full of hope.* (emphasis added)[57]

Douglas John Hall writes in similar language:

> God meets, takes on, takes into God's *own* being, the burden of our suffering, not by a show of force which could only destroy the sinner with the sin, but by assuming a solidary responsibility for the contradictory and confused admixture that is our life. God incarnate and crucified bears with us and for us the 'weight of sin' that is the root cause of our suffering, and that we cannot assume in our brokenness.[58]

Like Jürgen Moltmann, Douglas John Hall argues powerfully that only the persistent vulnerability of love can transform human lives. If the divine will were suppressive power intent upon the eradication of

---

[57]Moltmann, *The Crucified God*, 248.

[58]Douglas John Hall, *God and Human Suffering: An Exercise in the Theology of the Cross* (Minneapolis: Augsburg Publishing House, 1986), 113 (hereafter cited as *God and Human Suffering*).

lovelessness, enmity and other expressions of sin, then suppressive power would necessitate the annihilation of human will and therefore humanity. "There is no <u>sword</u> that can cut away sin without killing the sinner."[59]

In order to explore the ineffectiveness of divine suppressive power to save the sinner, Hall observes that there are human situations in which power is totally ineffective. For example, "Who through power tactics, can eliminate the self-destroying habits of a son or daughter?" Who can force the beloved to return love? However, powerful love, willing to be vulnerable rather than destroy, can love in spite of the indifference, rejection, and repudiation and can penetrate through them. That quality of love has the possibility of transforming people from within. A son or daughter, loved unconditionally, may experience new life; a lost love may return. The powerful love of God incarnate in the Cosmic Crucified has done precisely this, thereby drawing through persistent persuasion the most recalcitrant sinner unto himself. The Apostle Paul experienced that. "While we still were sinners Christ died for us" (Rom 5:8); therefore, the "love of Christ controls (RSV) (constrains, urges us on [NRSV]); because we are convinced that one has died for all . . . And he died for all, so that those who live might live no longer for themselves, but for him who died and was raised for them" (2 Cor 5:14-15).

Salvation is not grounded in divine, coercive imperial power which crushes opposition to God; rather salvation is derived from divine power willing to love, serve, agonize, and die in order that broken, sinful humanity might have life. "Here is the lamb of God that takes away the sin of the world" (Jn 1:29) ". . . this is love not that we loved God, but that [God] loved us and sent his Son to be the atoning sacrifice for our sins" (1 Jn 4:10).

Since Jesus Christ crucified is bedrock for the mission of the church, God's costly and unconditional love, offering forgiveness of sins in Jesus' name, will be at the heart of everything we do and say. God's persevering love in Jesus Christ is also the power and possibility of our own life and mission. God promises that in spite of ourselves we are usable and enables us to participate in the mission of God as disciples of the crucified Jesus.

In Pauline terms, justification, being right with God, is God's gift made possible through the infinite suffering of God and the crucified Jesus. "They are now justified by his grace as a gift, through the redemption that is in Christ Jesus" (Rom 3:24). The privilege and peculiar vocation of the

---

[59]Hall, *God and Human Suffering*, 98.

church as Jesus' community of disciples is to share the good news of forgiveness, justification, in Jesus Christ crucified, the good news of the cosmic shepherd who lays down his life for his sheep (John 10).

This understanding of the atonement and justification is the basis of our later contrast between costly grace in the gospel and merciful justice in the Qur'an.

D.   Jesus the Cosmic Crucified: The Continuing Suffering-with-Us God

Jesus crucified and risen reveals that God is passionately involved with broken people and vulnerable unto death for their salvation.

However, the Bible does not say that Jesus' death on the cross was God's original and only participation in human brokenness and suffering. Rather, according to the biblical faith, it is very clear that the suffering of the Cosmic Crucified is rooted in the suffering-with-us God who participated in the suffering of the ancient Hebrew slaves (Ex 3:7-8) and who will continue to participate in human suffering until that day when every tear shall be wiped away and death will be no more.   God's suffering love is not tangential to history.   It is not immersed in history for a few moments on Golgotha; rather, God's suffering love is immersed in human existence from the fall of Adam into sin and brokenness until that future when all tears will pass away (Rv 21:4).

Douglas John Hall writes: "Behind the 'must' of Jesus' passion there is the 'must' of the divine *agape*—and it is visible all the way from Eden!"[60]

First, it is essential to note that Jesus' own suffering as the crucified is rooted in and preceded by God's suffering-with-us love incarnate in Jesus: Jesus' death on Golgotha is preceded by the agonizing cries of Jesus for those who would not listen to God's prophetic word.   These cries are rooted in the broken heart of Jesus and of God.   "Jerusalem, Jerusalem, the city that kills the prophets and stones those who are sent to it!   How often have I desired to gather your children together as a hen gathers her brood under her wings, and you were not willing!" (Lk 13:34).   As Jesus approached Jerusalem for the last time, Luke reports:

> As he came near and saw the city, he wept over it, saying, "If you, even you, had only recognized on this day the things that make for peace!" (Lk 19:41).

---

[60]Hall, *God and Human Suffering*, 109.

Jesus the Cosmic Crucified suffered with those with whom he lived and suffered because of those with whom he lived long before he was hung on Calvary. The Gospels often state that Jesus looked with compassion on his contemporaries. Compassion literally means to suffer with, to love so deeply that one agonizes with someone. The Greek and Hebrew words lying behind the English translation have similar meanings. "When [Jesus] saw the crowds, he had compassion for them, because they were harassed and helpless, like sheep without a shepherd" (Mt 9:36; Mt 14:14, 15:32, 20:34). In theological terms we confess that God's incarnation in Jesus precedes and is the presupposition of the Cosmic Crucified's vulnerability unto death, the heart of the atonement.

The biblical tradition also reflects glimpses of God's compassion, suffering-with-us love, in the Old Testament. God's suffering-with-us love incarnate in Jesus is preceded by God's compassionate presence among the people of God portrayed in the Old Testament. Terence E. Fretheim has written a remarkable book entitled *The Suffering of God: An Old Testament Perspective.*[61] Fretheim states, "It can reasonably be claimed that the idea of a God who suffered with his people had its roots in the Exodus and in the subsequent reflections on the significance of that event."[62] He notes particularly Exodus 3:7-8 (cf. 2:23-25):

> Then the Lord said, "I have observed the misery of my people who are in Egypt; I have heard their cry on account of their taskmasters; Indeed, I know their sufferings, and I have come down to deliver them from the Egyptians."

Fretheim explains the significance of the verbs, *see, hear, know*, indicating that they, particularly *know*, emerge not only from experience but "intimate experience." "God is depicted here as one who is intimately involved in the suffering of the people."[63]

> God is thus portrayed not as a king dealing with an issue at some distance, nor even as one who sends a subordinate to cope with a problem, nor as one who issues an edict designed to alleviate the suffering. God sees the suffering from the inside; God does not look

---

[61]Fretheim, The Suffering of God: An Old Testament Perspective (Philadelphia: Fortress Press, 1984) (hereafter cited as *The Suffering of God*).

[62]Fretheim, *The Suffering of God*, 127.

[63]Fretheim, *The Suffering of God*, 128.

at it from the outside, as through a window. God is internally related to the suffering of the people. God enters fully into the hurtful situation and makes it his own. Yet, while God suffers with the people, God is not powerless to do anything about it.[64]

Another moving passage describing God as weeping for the land of God's people is found in Jeremiah 9:10:

I will take up [NRSV footnote, Hebrew text] weeping and wailing for the mountains, and a lamentation for the pastures of the wilderness, because they are laid waste so that no one passes through, and the lowing of cattle is not heard; both the birds of the air and the animals have fled and are gone.

In Jeremiah, God in love-wrath is compelled to purge Israel for its own sake; but God is with the suffering Israel and shares the pain of its purging.[65] Another perspective of God's participation in the pain of God's people is found in Isaiah's song of God's vineyard, Israel. God plants a vineyard, God's people, and God carefully watches over God's children, God's pleasant planting. God "expected justice, but saw bloodshed; righteousness, but heard a cry! (Is 5:7). Once again God creates a people, watches over a people, listens to a people and as a result, knows their bloodshed and cries and participates in them. In compassion, God cries, "Woe to those who cause the bloodshed and the cries." God's wrath is an expression of God's compassionate involvement in people's lives and in God's desire that they share justice and righteousness, that they have life.

Kosuke Koyama, writing in what he calls a Buddhist culture of tranquility, states that to speak of God's wrath in that context is a scandal. Disciplined monks, like the Buddha, are "free from wrath, the anti-Nirvanic emotion." In contrast, the biblical God is so passionately involved in people's lives (in history) that God shares the pain of injustice and brokenness. It is God's love (*agape*) that loves so deeply that God's righteous wrath wills to purge and transform cultures, nations and peoples.[66]

The biblical tradition sees the suffering-with-us God present and active before the incarnation and Jesus' crucifixion and also continuing after the death and resurrection of Jesus.

---

[64]Fretheim, *The Suffering of God*, 128.

[65]Fretheim, *The Suffering of God*; see chapters 8 and 9 for an excellent discussion of this topic.

[66]Koyama, *Waterbuffalo Theology*, chapters 9, 11 and 13.

This passionate solidarity of God with human suffering, continues until the close of the age. This continuing compassion is powerfully portrayed in Jesus' parable of the last judgment in Matthew 25:31-46. In that parable the Son of Man who presides over the judgment says, "I was hungry and you gave me food, I was thirsty and you gave me something to drink. . . . I was a stranger and you did not welcome me, naked and you did not give me clothing . . . as you did or did not do it to one of the least of these, you did not do it to me." Of deepest significance in this parable is the announcement that God in God's agent of judgment, the Cosmic Crucified, is so intimately wrapped up in human existence that God actually experienced the pain of hunger, nakedness, and loneliness as well as being fed, clothed, and comforted with God's children. This passionate solidarity with people will continue "to the close of the age."

Like the Old Testament, the New Testament speaks of God's continuing suffering because of humanity's continuing sin and rebellion. God still grieves when people turn away from God and walk into their self-chosen darkness. Jesus' parable of the prodigal son portrays a father who exuberantly rejoices when a lost son returns home. Joy bursts forth from a father who had agonized with his son in his absence and who "was filled with compassion (suffering-with-us love)" when he saw him approaching from afar (Lk 15:20). The joy and suffering in heaven (God and angels) (Lk 15:10) portrayed in this parable of Jesus describes a God who, until all tears are wiped away, continues to participate in the agony of those who are wayward family and yet beloved. A passage in Ephesians picks up this theme in an exhortation to live within the will of God: "And *do not grieve* the Holy Spirit of God, with which you were marked with a seal for the day of redemption" (Eph 4:30).

In previous paragraphs, references to Israel's brokenness and suffering and to Matthew 25 imply that brokenness, oppression and suffering are physical as well as spiritual and psychological. Psychological, social, and spiritual brokenness and suffering are obviously real, torturous and devastating. The spiritual agony of persons who know that they have betrayed God and themselves, the loneliness of life when sin tears peoples lives apart, the hopelessness that can be experienced when those most loved are suddenly crushed or gone, the meaninglessness of life when purpose disappears—all are experiences of brokenness, inner pain and suffering. The incarnation is God's promise that God participates in that psychological, social and spiritual pain. Hunger, thirst, nakedness, the denial of freedom, imprisonment are also experiences of brokenness and pain. The promise of Jesus crucified is that God has descended into the depths of the sum total of corporate agony. A theology of the cross is rooted in God's passionate, costly involvement in the pain and suffering of cosmic and human life. "The Word became flesh and lived among us . . ." (Jn 1:14). That in itself is "good news" when all visible signs point to the absence of God or the distance of God.

Christians who are citizens of the U.S.A. and members of an affluent church will perhaps be surprised that much of the two-thirds world will find gospel (good news) in the very announcement that God incarnate in Jesus Christ is present in the midst of the world's poverty and oppression and that God in Christ continues, as in ancient Israel, to hear the cries of God's broken and suffering people. In Jesus' parable of the last judgment (Mt 25:31ff) that is exactly what Jesus promises. It is the promise of the Cosmic Crucified that whenever a child is hungry, Christ shares the hunger; whenever a mother weeps at the death of her child, Christ weeps; whenever a person is maligned or cursed, Christ is maligned and cursed; whenever a human is beaten to death Christ dies again. That in and of itself is gospel when the marks of life within poverty, oppression and death are read to mean the absence or distance of God. C. S. Song movingly writes, "In suffering or in death, namely, in the situation of utter despair and emptiness, we are not alone. We do not suffer alone and die alone".[67]

It is essential to note that many countries with Muslim majorities are also countries that rate among the poorest in the world; for example, Afghanistan (99% Muslim, ranks 3rd); Bangladesh (85% Muslim, ranks 23rd); Mali (90% Muslim, ranks 5th); Somalia (99% Muslim, ranks 7th). These Muslim peoples have a right to hear of the God who in Christ died for their sins and also the God who in Christ shares their poverty, their dreams and their cries.

In the previous section, "The Cosmic-Crucified: Divine Vulnerability Unto Death for the Ungodly," the once-for-allness of Jesus' atoning death was emphasized. In this section, the "continuing suffering-with-us God" has been focused upon. It is possible that someone may interpret this as contradictory; however, it is also possible that the gospel is so rich and has such depth, that two or more affirmations are essential to the Christian witness. The Lutheran tradition of both . . . and (*simul . . . et*) certainly recognizes this. We are both sinners and saints. At the Lord's table we receive both bread and the body of Christ. It is faithfulness to the biblical tradition that compels one to say both: Christ died once for all, and the Cosmic Crucified continues to suffer with and for his people.

This presentation of a theology of the cross affirms that Jesus was crucified for our sins once for all, and at the same time, through Jesus, we look into the heart of God and find a compassionate God who in love has

[67]Song, *Third Eye Theology*, 184 cf Rom 8:38-39.

agonized with the human community from the origins of the human race and will continue to participate in human suffering until that future moment when all tears shall be wiped away. It is therefore not surprising that one sees the marks or footsteps of that costly pain-love of God in Exodus, Hosea, Jeremiah and Isaiah or may even find glimpses of it in Buddhist reflections on the *bodhisattva*, the person who sacrifices *nirvana* in order to continue to share human suffering until others also know the way out of the pain of human existence. This double affirmation of the finality of Jesus Christ and the continuing universal presence and activity of God even outside the community of the body of Christ is also clearly stated in DGM Commitment 3. "Even though this incarnate God is unknown to people, the Triune God is already present and active in their lives and desires that the depths of God's saving love in Christ might be known by them."

Trinitarian theology implies that God active within Israel and incarnate in the Cosmic Crucified is the same God who created the cosmos; permeates every corner of an expanding 30 billion light-year universe; continually upholds, creates and orders the cosmos; and the same God who at some future point will bring all cosmic history to God's intended fulfillment.[68]

If I were an artist, I would like to paint on a gigantic scale an image that would capture something of the infinity and depth of space and galaxies, broken humanity, and God's saving act of grace in Christ. Concretely on a hill would hang on a cross a lonely, tortured figure whose shadow was cast across a multitude of shattered human faces and stretching out to the boundaries of space and time. It is a trinitarian faith that believes that the cross of the Cosmic Crucified lies within the heart of God and therefore the heart of the universe. A trinitarian faith believes this because the resurrection and the Holy Spirit affirm that God has identified Godself in the crucified Jesus and therefore God has been incarnate and revealed in Jesus Christ. Jesus Christ becomes for faith the window through which one looks into the heart of the universe. D. M. Baillie in his book *God Was In Christ* quotes Charles Allen Dinsmore who wrote: "'There was a cross in the heart of God . . . before there was one planted on the green hill outside Jerusalem.'"[69]

---

[68]The following three paragraphs are from a letter written August 27, 1990, to an ELCA missionary and copied to several others who challenged this double affirmation of the suffering of God.

[69]D. M. Baillie, *God Was In Christ: An Essay on Incarnation and Atonement* (New York: Charles Scribner's Sons, 1955), 194.

This faith announces that Jesus crucified and risen is already present in the world's agony before the gospel is announced. This faith says, "Let me tell you of that one whom you do not yet truly or fully know." It insists on saying to Hindus, Buddhists and Muslims, "Let me tell you what has already happened in Jesus Christ for you. The God to whom you pray and who has heard your prayers went through hell itself for you and is in your own hell with you." It is this witness which creates faith in order that all may live in that New God-given Messianic Age inaugurated in Jesus Christ.

To put all this briefly, the announcement of Good News from the perspective of this statement is not only a divine linguistic event creating faith; it is a divine linguistic event creating faith in a divine cosmic fact and reality present and active before it is announced. It is present and active because creation and salvation through the death of the Cosmic Crucified are cosmic realities that precede the presence and proclamation of the gospel.

Affirmation of the suffering-with-us God is an affirmation of continuing passionate involvement rather than distance or indifference in regard to God. We will discuss later that the God revealed and known through Jesus, the Cosmic Crucified, is not acceptable to most Muslims with whom we wish to engage. For most Sunni Muslims, suffering is not appropriate to the divine. Kenneth Cragg writes, "Behind this instinctive sense of things theological in the Qur'an and in Islam lies the conviction that there can be no place for suffering in deity. For 'suffering' seems to imply some external source inflicting it . . . some inferiority that can be 'subject' to restraint."[70] God as Immanuel and Compassion, as suffering-with-us Love even into the incarnation and unto vulnerability to death, is not fitting to divine sovereignty and glory, according to Muslim thought. This is one of the most problematic and difficult discussions that emerges from Christian-Muslim conversations. Conversations on revelation, salvation, and surrender to the will of God (Islam), return again and again to this point. The point must never be surrendered; it marks a striking difference between Christian and Muslim understandings of God. I have always found it striking that Christian scholars of Islam like Kenneth Cragg, Willem Bijlefeld, and Harold Vogelaar become aware of this distinction and that awareness has led them to a deep appreciation of this motif within the gospel message.

---

[70]Kenneth Cragg, *Muhammad and the Christian: A Question of Response* (Maryknoll, New York: Orbis, 1984), 138.

Our discussions with Buddhists will take an entirely different path. Buddhists see suffering or impermanence as the essential mark of human existence. That is simply the basic reality of life from which one seeks release. One Buddhist scholar expressed deep appreciation for this missiology of the cross, because it takes human brokenness very seriously; however, he thought reference to Jesus' finality was invalid. Another observed that God is irrelevant to the Buddhist quest for release. With Muslims, one discusses the nature of God. With Buddhists, one must begin at a more fundamental level, namely, God.

E.   Jesus the Cosmic Crucified and the Messianic Struggle for Life in the Midst of Death

Gustav Aulen in his book, *Christus Victor*, interprets Jesus' death and resurrection in cosmic, dualistic terms.[71] Jesus Christ dies in a cosmic battle between the Kingdom of God and the demonic "principalities and powers." Jesus' death and resurrection are God's ultimate triumph over the powers of sin, death and the devil. It is essential to reclaim this conflict-victory theme for an understanding of the totality of God's saving, atoning work; however, the conflict-victory theme must be radically interpreted in the light of the Cosmic Crucified. The nature of the combat must be seen in Jesus as the powerful yet vulnerable-to-death prophet. The conflict-victory theme can never be understood in terms of our contemporary understanding of might and power nor our seeming eternal quest for invulnerability. Only the life and death of Jesus defines the conflict and the power. The conflict is a struggle that God's *will* might be done on earth even as it is done in heaven. The power is self-giving, serving love, which is willing to be vulnerable to death in order that newness of life might be realized.

The New Testament document Luke-Acts describes the cosmic duel in Kingdom and Spirit terms. Jesus announced the nearness and arrival of the promised reign/kingdom of God. The prophetic promises of Isaiah are fulfilled (Lk 4:18-21, 7:22-23); the disciples have seen what prophets and kings had longed to see (Lk 10:23); the kingdom's power set captives free (Lk 11:20); and a new age of the kingdom had dawned (Lk 16:16) and was already in the midst of them (Lk 17:20-21). The arrival of God's kingdom, empowered by the Spirit of God (Jesus' birth, Lk 1:35; baptism, Lk 3:21-22; ministry, Lk 4:18) brought kingdom life and light into the realm of

---

[71]Gustav Aulen, *Christus Victor* (New York: Macmillan, 1931).

62   *The Word and the Way of the Cross*

death and darkness. The encounter between the kingdom and the satanic powers (Lk 11:14-23) resulted in the ultimate combat between life and death. The cosmic triumph of God over sin, death and the devil cost Jesus' life. He hung on Golgotha in the darkness and the wind. On the third day God raised Jesus from the dead. The Cosmic Crucified now sits at God's right hand (Acts 2)!

Aulen sees Martin Luther as a primary interpreter of this "classical" view of cosmic conflict and victory in Jesus Christ.[72] In the great Reformation hymn, Luther wrote:

> A mighty fortress is our God,
>   A sword and shield victorious;
> He breaks the cruel oppressor's rod
>   And wins salvation glorious.
> The old satanic foe
>   Has sworn to work us woe!
> With craft and dreadful might
>   He arms himself to fight.
> On earth he has no equal.
>
> No strength of ours can match his might!
>   We would be lost, rejected.
> But now a champion comes to fight,
>   Whom God himself elected.
> You ask who this may be?
>   The Lord of hosts is he!
> Christ Jesus, mighty Lord,
>   God's only Son, adored.
> He holds the field victorious.[73]

In *Luther and Liberation: A Latin American Perspective*[74] Walter Altmann asserts in a similar way that Luther's Christology is dynamic and combative:

---

[72] Large Catechism and Small Catechism in *The Book of Concord*, the Second Article of the Creed and its meaning (see both), 345,413-415.

[73] Copyright©1978 *Lutheran Book of Worship*. Reprinted by permission of Augsburg Fortress.

[74] Walter Altmann, *Luther and Liberation: A Latin American Perspective* (Minneapolis: Fortress Press, 1992).

This is especially clear when his theology concentrates on the cross, the point of confluence in the historical and cosmic battle between evil and righteousness, curse and blessing, and death and life. Here, there is no defeated resignation but rather shared and redemptive suffering. The dead Jesus of popular Latin American veneration may be the expression of resigned and impotent suffering (and may also be an image that helps people survive under oppression), but Christ-crucified, as interpreted by Luther, is divine love's combatant. His cross is not defeat, but rather the victorious culmination of an all-out battle. Hence Christus victor—victorious Christ.[75]

Then Altmann writes, "Throughout the course of the history of the Lutheran church, the combative aspect has been forgotten along with the necessity of following Jesus Christ in his path, of joining Jesus Christ in his kenosis, his emptying out."[76] Altmann, who has deep roots within the Lutheran tradition, has been deeply influenced by his Latin American context, marked by poverty and oppression, and shares deeply in the Latin American churches' struggle to relate the gospel of Jesus Christ to that situation. With other Latin American theologians, Altmann understands Jesus' crucifixion as the outcome of a liberation struggle waged between Jesus and his religious and political contemporaries. However, this historical conflict is rooted in the cosmic conflict between the kingdom of God and the powers of darkness[77].

Leonardo Boff writes:

Through his life and message, Jesus, acting in the name of God, strove to inculcate in human beings a spirit that would never cause crosses for others; and now he himself hangs on a cross. His cross is not the result of an arbitrary whim on God's part. It results from the way in which the world is organized. Sinfully closed in upon itself, the world rejected the God of Jesus and eliminated Jesus

---

[75]Altmann, *Luther and Liberation: A Latin American Perspective*, 24.

[76]Altmann, *Luther and Liberation: A Latin American Perspective*, 25.

[77]Gustavo Gutierrez, *A Theology of Liberation: History, Politics and Salvation* (Maryknoll, New York: Orbis Books, 1973), 228-232. See also Song, *Third Eye Theology*, 218ff.

himself. The execution of Jesus is the greatest sin ever committed because it stands in opposition to God's will, which is to establish the Kingdom in the midst of the creation.[78]

God or the kingdom of God was embodied in Jesus. The powers of darkness were embodied in priests, scholars, governors, kings and throngs. Boff writes, "They were actors in a drama that went much deeper than they themselves. The real protagonists were the Evil One and the sin of the world; they were the ones ultimately responsible for Jesus' death."[79] Jesus as bearer of the kingdom preached good news to the poor, proclaimed forgiveness to the damned, healed the sick, liberated the possessed. However, Jesus' messianic ministry enraged the religious and scholarly elite and aroused the hostility of the political powers. In other words, it was Jesus' struggle to bring God's life-giving kingdom into the midst of death that infuriated those who embodied the powers of darkness: the powers of religious, social, economic, and political oppression.

There were specific historical reasons why Jesus battled the powers of darkness that ruled Galilee and Judea, and there were specific historical reasons why Jesus was nailed to a cross. On behalf of the kingdom's struggle for life, Jesus prophetically challenged the faith, values, and traditions of his contemporaries. "Though Jesus was more than a prophet, it was his prophetic call to change that caused his death."[80] It was the struggle for kingdom-life and Jesus' prophetic challenge of the voices of darkness that hung Jesus in the dust and the wind. If we are to witness to Jesus Christ crucified, it is essential that we explore the relationship between Jesus' death at the hands of his enemies and Jesus' struggle on behalf of God's life-giving kingdom.[81]

We will explore Jesus' prophetic ministry in some detail because our Muslim and Buddhist friends are often fascinated by Jesus' life and mission. They may have absolutely no interest in Augustine, Thomas Aquinas, Luther or Calvin, but they often desire "to see Jesus," and it is in

---

[78]Leonardo Boff, *Way of the Cross-Way of Justice* (Maryknoll, New York: Orbis Books, 1982), 89. Boff wrote this fascinating book, at the end of seven years of christological study and six major publications dealing with Christology.

[79]Boff, *Way of the Cross-Way of Justice*, ix.

[80]Marcus J. Borg, *Jesus: A New Vision* (San Francisco: Harper & Row, 1987), 184.

[81]The theological focus upon liberation within the context of poverty and oppression has literally encircled the globe: Black theology in Africa, Minjing theology in Korea, and Dalit theology in India. The theme has permeated almost every theological movement and confessional family in the world.

Jesus that they will see the presence and action of the kingdom of God as God contests with the powers of darkness. This missiology of the cross places Jesus' prophetic ministry of the approaching kingdom of God in an integral relationship to the cross and God's vulnerability unto death for the ungodly.

1. Life for the Damned

Jesus' unconditional, self-giving, seeking love for those stigmatized as lost or "damned"; Jesus' willingness to converse and eat with them; and his freedom to announce grace and forgiveness in their midst astounded Jesus' contemporaries. It is not surprising that the Gospel of Luke concludes:

> "Thus it is written, that the Messiah is to suffer and to rise from the dead on the third day, and that repentance and forgiveness of sins is to be proclaimed in his name to all nations." (Lk 24:46-47)

Some of Jesus' contemporaries were not only astounded but were appalled and infuriated by Jesus' words and actions. Jesus violated and desecrated their understanding of God's will and intended order for God's people.

There seems to be a universal principle at work within religious people of the world. They are always drawing circles around God. There are those inside the circle named the elect, the called, the blessed, the saved of God, and there are those outside the circle named the nonelected, those who are outside the blessing and salvation of God, the damned. Jesus makes it very clear that when religious people draw circles demarking insiders and outsiders in terms of moral standards, religious rectitude, race, or sex, one can always know that Jesus will be on the other side of the line, insisting that God wills in love to embrace the whole human community.[82]

In *Jesus: A New Vision* Marcus Borg describes what he considers to be the historical and sociological origins of this religious tendency among Jesus' contemporaries. He believes that many within the Jewish community saw their religious traditions and values being threatened by hellenistic culture and Roman political power. In order to prevent the destruction of their own way of life, they developed what Borg designates "the politics of

---

[82]The picture of Jesus being on the other side of the line comes from lectures and conversations with Dr. Duane Priebe of Wartburg Theological Seminary, Dubuque, Iowa.

holiness," which emphasized "God was holy and Israel was to be holy."[83]
The Pharisees were leading advocates of this holiness movement focussing
on religious and ritual purity and tithing. Failure to live in accordance with
holiness norms resulted in ostracism, and "the major vehicle of social and
religious ostracism was the refusal of table fellowship."[84] In contrast to the
"politics of holiness," Borg sees Jesus develop the "politics of compassion"
marked by, among other things, banqueting with outcasts, association with
women, good news for the poor and peace advocacy within a revolutionary
hate environment.[85] An awareness of these universal and particular
holiness norms are essential as one attempts to understand the radical
message and mission of Jesus and the violent opposition Jesus eventually
aroused.

Luke collects a number of stories and parables of Jesus that reflect
Jesus' radical grace and the criticism and resentment Jesus' ministry began
to arouse. There is the "woman of the city, who was a sinner," who wept
at Jesus' feet, anointing Jesus' feet with oil (Lk 7:36-50). This took place
as Jesus was dining in the home of a Pharisee named Simon. Imagine
what brought this woman into the midst of the religious authorities who
despised her. Could it have been that Jesus was the first person who
spoke of God who also had spoken to her—talked to her as if she were
someone of value, someone for whom God cared? Might she have heard
him tell the parable of the prodigal son (Lk 15:11-24)? Whatever brought
her there, the miracle of the story is that she knew that she could trust
Jesus, that Jesus would not ridicule her and send her away. In gratitude
she wept at his feet, and she heard him say, "Your sins are forgiven; go
in peace." That is bringing life into the midst of death, life to the damned.

Jesus' saving action and words were immediately contested. The
Pharisees contended that a man of God, a prophet, would recognize what
sort of woman this was touching him (Lk 7:39). People of God, people
set apart for that which is holy, were not to touch, flesh against flesh, those
who had defiled themselves in sin. To Jesus she was not the profaned, the
sinner, the damned; she was the wayward child of God who had come
home, one for whom the Father had wept and of whom he had dreamed,
one who was to be swept into God's open and embracing arms. To the
Pharisees she was an irresponsible and degenerate woman who would not
experience the presence and forgiveness of God.

[83]Borg, *Jesus: A New Vision*, 86.

[84]Borg, *Jesus: A New Vision*, 89.

[85]Borg, *Jesus: A New Vision*, 131-141.

Luke in chapter 19 tells the story of Zacchaeus, the crooked tax collector and political collaborator from Jericho (Lk 19:1-10). Zacchaeus was rich, despised by the patriotic Jewish community for both his greed and his willingness to cooperate with the Roman invaders and by the religious community because of failure to live by its holiness code. Perhaps he despised himself as thoroughly as did the patriotic and religious community. Something compelled him to look for Jesus, and he was filled with joy when Jesus said that he wanted to spend the day with him. There was an immediate reaction within the crowd. "They all murmured, 'he has gone in to be the guest of one who is a sinner.'" Jesus said, "He too is a son of Abraham."

Like Matthew and Mark, Luke also relates how Jesus called Levi, a tax collector, to be his disciple (Lk 5:27-32). Levi gave a banquet attended by a large crowd of tax collectors and others sitting at the table. Again the Pharisees and Scribes were complaining, "Why do you eat and drink with the tax collectors and sinners?" Jesus' practice of banqueting with sinners led to the accusation that he was "a glutton and drunkard, a friend of tax collectors and sinners" (Lk 7:34). Jesus responded to the questions and charges by saying he had come to seek the lost (Lk 19:10), to call sinners to repentance (Lk 5:32), to announce the forgiveness of God (Lk 7:47). Jesus insisted that his message and mission was molded by God and necessary to kingdom-life.

Jesus asserted that God was with those relegated to "the damned" and that God's incomprehensible forgiveness was there. Outside the temple, the synagogue, the authoritarian ministry, the traditional religious community, God was there sharing the pain of the ostracized, crossing lines and destroying walls. Jesus defended his evangelical witness, asserting that God, like a shepherd, seeks for lost sinners (Lk 15:3-7) and God, like a woman overwhelmed with the excitement of finding one lost coin from her wedding dowry, rejoices when one lost sinner is found (Lk 15:8-10). Jesus announced that a tax collector, defiled, lost and "damned," was loved and forgiven/justified while weeping before God alone in the temple (Lk 18:9-14). This proclamation was grace for the damned. It was a struggle for life in the midst of death. It resulted in a costly conflict for which Jesus would finally lose his life. Oppressive religious traditions and hierarchical authorities were not about to step aside without a struggle. They would eventually insist that this false messianic prophet must die, and Jesus, walking the vulnerable way required by his Father in heaven, would hang outside the walls of the holy city.

Unconditional grace and forgiveness, rooted in the pain-love of God, are at the heart of the gospel. They are at the heart of the proclamation that Jesus is the Cosmic Crucified; they were at the heart of Jesus' own kingdom message and mission. This gospel must be our gospel!

> But God, who is rich in mercy, out of the great love with which he loved us even when we were dead through our trespasses, made us alive together with Christ—by grace you have been saved–. . . and this is not your own doing; it is the gift of God. (Eph 2:4-10)

This message astounded Jesus' contemporaries. Some received it with awe-filled joy; others resented the seeming "cheap and unjust grace" (Mt 20:1-16). The message still astounds us and often is limited by us as we prescribe the limits of God's costly pain-love. As we converse with Muslims and Buddhists we should not be surprised that we often find the same skepticism about an understanding of God which insists that justice must be understood within the context of God's unconditional suffering love rather than seeing compassion through the lens of justice.

2. Good News to the Poor

In the Gospel of Luke, Jesus began his ministry with the words:

> "The Spirit of the Lord is upon me, because he has anointed me to bring good news to the poor. He has sent me to proclaim release to the captives and recovery of sight to the blind, to let the oppressed go free, to proclaim the year of the Lord's favor."
> (Lk 4:18-19)

This messianic passage from Isaiah 61, which Jesus says is fulfilled in his ministry, begins with the announcement that good news is preached to the poor. I believe many of us are beginning to realize what this means—why it is incredibly good news!

Human existence is marked by suffering and death. Often those who experience most deeply the tragic pain of life are those who live in poverty and under oppression. Those who live in poverty often experience hunger. They give birth to children only to see them grow malnourished and subject to disease. They see opportunities for themselves and their children limited by their financial resources or society's prejudices. They experience the cold of winter without sufficient fuel. They often leave their homes and families in order to earn wages to feed and clothe their families. They experience the loneliness of human isolation, whether it be as blind beggars on the streets of Calcutta or refugees on the Somalian desert. They are usually the victims of economic and political warfare. They are the ones exploited by social-political structures grounded in greed and prejudice. They are the ones who are ignored, forgotten, ridiculed, and abused by the world's rich and powerful. They are the ones who often conclude that God has also forgotten them. Everything surrounding people living in poverty and under oppression suggests "God is not with you! God is not here! If God lives, God has forgotten you, ignores you—or even worse, God is punishing you!"

There seems to be something universal about what Hindu people call the law of *karma*. *Karma* means that for every human action, there is a cosmic reaction. Evil actions always result in cosmic judgment. Good actions always result in cosmic reward. This karmic law is seen working through the principle of reincarnation. If one is living in poverty or afflicted by leprosy, one knows that one is experiencing the consequences of evil actions performed in a previous existence. If one lives in health and prosperity, one lives with the consequences of previous good actions. One always knows that one is getting exactly what one deserves.

Jesus' contemporaries had similar thoughts within their religious culture. When Jesus' disciples saw a blind man, they asked, "Who sinned, this man or his parents?" (Jn 9:2). When a tower of Siloam fell upon people, Jesus' contemporaries immediately assumed that they were greater sinners than those who had been spared (Lk 13:1-5). Likewise, Jesus' contemporaries assumed that health and wealth were a sign of God's blessing. Jesus left his disciples astounded when he said that it was practically impossible for a rich man to be saved. Who then, they asked can possibly be saved? (Mk 10:17-27). Millions of people still accept the idea that poverty and oppression are God's punishment for sin, while wealth is God's reward for righteousness.[86] In its most blatant form this idea was expounded by South African white Christians who taught that black people were cursed by God and intended to be the servants of white people until the close of history. The Reverend Zephania Kameeta, a black Namibian pastor, put that curse in contemporary language with the words, "We have been taught all our lives that we are God's mistake."

Millions of people not only suffer and die in poverty and under oppression, but they suffer and die believing that their poverty not only signifies the absence of God and the silence of God, but possibly, the judgment of God. Into that tragic pain-filled world Jesus comes to share and bear the world's suffering. He announces the arrival and presence of

---

[86]Borg, *Jesus: A New Vision*, 82.

the kingdom of God in himself (Lk 10:23-24; 11:20; 17:21), and he promises that the kingdom of God comes to turn the world upside down. Contrary to all the signs which might indicate that the poor and oppressed have been forgotten or condemned Jesus promises:

> "Blessed are you who are poor, for yours is the kingdom of God. Blessed are you who are hungry now, for you will be filled. Blessed are you who weep now, for you will laugh." (Lk 6:20-21)

Strange as it might seem, this promise of life for the poor was one of the factors that contributed to the death of Jesus. Jesus' contemporary critics insisted that poverty, sickness, and death were signs of God's judgment. Jesus contradicted that. They also believed that health and prosperity were signs of their right (inside) relationship with God. Jesus vehemently denied that also. To the contrary, Jesus cried:

> "Woe to you who are rich, for you have received your consolation. Woe to you who are full now, for you will be hungry. Woe to you who are laughing now, for you will mourn and weep." (Lk 6:24-25)

Health and wealth were no assurance of God's blessing. Instead, Jesus saw them as likely signs that something was tragically wrong in human life (Lk 16:19-31). Jesus saw in wealth the possibility that humanity might place their ultimate confidence in wealth rather than God (Lk 12:13-21). He also saw wealth as a God-given resource to be shared with all humanity, particularly the poor. Jesus constantly challenged people of wealth to share God's resources of which they were stewards or to be judged as those outside the kingdom of God (Mt 25:31-46; Mk 10:17-27; Lk 12:32-34; 14:12-14; 19:1-10). Jesus saw the wealthy torn between God and their wealth, and he said, "You cannot serve God and wealth" (Lk 16:13). Luke then comments, "The Pharisees, who were lovers of money, heard all this, and they ridiculed him." Knowing that their ridicule hid their inner rebellion Jesus replied, "You are those who justify yourselves in the sight of others; but God knows your hearts; for what is prized by human beings is an abomination in the sight of God" (Lk 16:14-15). No doubt the combat that hung Jesus in the dust and the wind was vigorously in process.

One of the theological miracles of the late twentieth century is the rediscovery of the biblical witness to God's particular concern for the poor and oppressed, "the preferential option for the poor."[87] It is not surprising that it was the Christian community living in poverty and under oppression that rediscovered this basic biblical motif. Persons living within poverty and oppression read the Bible with different eyes from most of us. Prophetic visions of justice, comfort for the oppressed, denunciations of tyranny normally missed by comfortable Christians of affluent societies leap from the page when read by Christians of Korea, India, Namibia, South Africa, and Latin America.

It is the poor and oppressed who are comforted and empowered by Jesus' blessings and woes. They hear from the prophets and the risen one that the political and economic forces that crush their lives are not the instruments of God. They are, rather, demonic structures that lie under the judgment of God. It is Jesus who promises that God's kingdom, contrary to all visible signs, has already grasped the poor, and God's future is God's gift to them. This gospel empowers people crushed by historical realities to live in God's marvelous light. People who have had their faces pushed into the dust and have been told that they are society's nobodies are suddenly, in Christ, somebody unique and special, the children of God! People who have questioned the value of their own existence suddenly in faith know themselves to be created in the image of God with value and gifts they have never dreamed of. Dalit theology, an Indian theology of the "crushed ones" or outcasts, emphasizes Hosea's theme, "Once you were no people of mine, now you are my people, children of the living God" (Hos 2:23). Dalit theology focuses on every human being as created in the image of God and therefore having divine value and potential gifts. It is this same liberating theme that has been seen by women who read the Bible with new eyes. Repentance from this perspective can been seen as dying to one's old self which denies one's God-given value and potential in order to be raised to a new empowered life of discipleship by the power of the gospel and the Holy Spirit. In the words of Desmond Tutu, this biblical faith, rediscovered by the world's marginalized, empowers the oppressed to stop shuffling their feet in the presence of the powerful and "look the chap in the eye and speak face to face."[88]

---

[87]Leonardo and Clodovis Boff, *Introducing Liberation Theology* (Maryknoll, New York: Orbis Books, 1987), chapters 2 and 3.

[88]Desmond Tutu, "The Theology of Liberation in Africa," in *African Theology en Route, Papers from the Pan-African Conference of Third World Theologians, December 17-23, 1977, Accra, Ghana,* Kofi Appiah-Kubi and Sergio Torres, eds. (Maryknoll, New York: Orbis Books, 1979), 168.

Out of that experience giants in the faith arise: persons who in Jesus' name continue his prophetic ministry; persons who are ridiculed, imprisoned, and tortured for righteousness' sake; persons who arise every morning to walk in Christ's way even though it may mean death; persons whom we must listen to and know in order that we might once again hear the call of Jesus to discipleship and be grasped by the power of his Spirit.

3. Healing the Sick and Liberating the Oppressed

Jesus' life-giving ministry touched the blind, the lame, the lepers, the deaf, the possessed, and the dead. Jesus gave them sight, made them walk, cleansed their skin, opened their eyes, unstopped their ears. His healing-liberating ministry set them free and gave them life. Jesus claimed that these were signs that the kingdom of God and God's Messiah were here (Lk 7:22; Is 29:18-19; 35:5-6) and the demonic powers were being deposed (Lk 11:14-23). Human lives were being healed, human bodies were being transformed, and the Spirit of God was the energizing power in the midst of that (Acts 10:38). Kingdom-life appeared in the midst of death. Jesus announced that the coming and the presence of God's kingdom was the fulfillment of the prophetic dreams of Israel. Prophets had dreamed that one day God would do a "new thing." The whole of creation would be restored (Is 11:1-9). Isaiah described this restored world:

> Then the eyes of the blind shall be opened, and the ears of the deaf unstopped; then the lame shall leap like a deer, and the tongue of the speechless sing for joy. For waters shall break forth in the wilderness, and streams in the desert. (Is 35:5-7)

Jesus announced that God had begun to do "a new thing." "Blessed are your eyes," said Jesus, for "many prophets and kings desired to see what you see, and did not see it" (Lk 10:23-24). The kingdom of God had been inaugurated.

The messianic dream was being fulfilled. Total fulfillment was still a future dream; however, the mustard seed had been planted, and the leaven was already at work in the loaf (Lk 13:18-21). The blind saw, the deaf heard, the poor had good news preached to them.

The healing-liberating ministry of Jesus was a mark of God's work of restoration and re-creation. God intends to transform the whole of creation—human bodies and minds as well as their souls. It is essential to see that Jesus' miracles and exorcisms were not just religious sideshows that somehow authenticated his message of forgiveness and the promise of eternal life. They were an essential part of Jesus' mission, which proclaimed God's presence and saving action in words of truth, healing of re-creation, and liberation of the demonically oppressed.

Participation in the mission of the crucified Jesus means that witness to the gospel takes the totality of human lives in all their relationships with utmost seriousness. If one is to witness to the Jesus of Scripture in the ghettos of the nations, one must be concerned about people's bodies–in other words, their health, their wages, their families, their contracts, as well as their personal life with God.

This dimension of Jesus' ministry is rooted in the Christian conviction that the God and Father of the Lord Jesus Christ is the creator of the heavens and the earth. Within the silence of eternity God speaks, and there is light and reality. God speaks, creation is, and it is good! Within the chaos of darkness there is life and order and truth. Humanity in rebellion distorts that beauty of life, which in God's eyes is good; however, the Bible insists that within the suffering and brokenness of life there are signs of God's original creativity, remnants of that which is good. Furthermore, the creative and redemptive power of God incarnate in the Cosmic Crucified continues to bring light and creativity into the darkness and death, and faith trusts that there will be one day a new heaven and a new earth. "God himself will be with them; he will wipe every tear from their eyes. Death will be no more" (Rv 21:3-4).

Paradoxically, it was the healing ministry of Jesus that once again brought Jesus into conflict with the religious establishment of his day. The conflict is illustrated by an incident in a synagogue on a sabbath (Mk 3:1-6). A man with a withered hand appeared. Jesus' critics watched carefully to see whether Jesus would heal him on this holy day. The context suggests that Jesus had healed on sabbath days in the past. Sharp lines were drawn between Jesus and his opponents. The religious authorities insisted that the sabbath day was a holy day on which work should not be done. Had not God said on the sabbath you shall do no work? (Ex 20:8-11). According to the hierarchy, priority had to be placed on religious tradition and practice.

By contrast, Jesus demanded that priority be placed on human pain, suffering, and need. Jesus confronted his critics with the fact that even they recognize that certain emergencies had to be taken care of on the sabbath: "Suppose one of you, has only one sheep and it falls into a pit on the sabbath; will you not lay hold of it and lift it out?" (Mt 12:11; Lk 14:6). Then Jesus said, "How much more valuable is a human being than a sheep!" (Mt 12:12). People are of value, ultimate value, in God's eyes.

If they suffer, that is a crisis that takes priority over religious tradition and ritual. On holy days one is called by God to save life, not destroy it (Mk 3:4).

Then Jesus grieved because of their hardness of heart and said, "Stretch out your hand," and the man's withered hand was restored, healed, re-created. After this the religious authorities held counsel with the Jewish politicians as to "how to destroy him" (Mk 3:6; Mt 12:14).

Jesus waged a running battle over God's priorities in life. The religious establishment said ritual and tradition took priority, even if it meant human suffering. Jesus claimed that God gave priority to the alleviation of human suffering. If there were conflicts between tradition and alleviation of suffering through the re-creation of life, Jesus had no doubt as to where God was in the debate. When his disciples were hungry on the sabbath, their hunger took priority over sabbath tradition (Mt 12:1-8). When evaluating the weightier matters of the law, mercy and justice took precedence over traditional religious observances (Mt 23:23). Jesus stood within a long prophetic tradition within Israel, in which mercy, righteousness, and justice for people were always prioritized ahead of religious ritual and tradition of any kind. The prophets had brought this word from the Lord:

> "I take no delight in your solemn assemblies. . . . Take away from me the noise of your songs; . . . But let justice roll down like waters, and righteousness like an ever-flowing stream." (Amos 5:21-24; Isaiah 1 and 58; Jeremiah 7)

Jesus was absolutely convinced that for God it was people that counted. God saw their afflictions, heard their cries, knew their suffering, and willed to restore and re-create them. Faithfulness to God would be indicated most clearly in sharing love and service with humanity. To Jesus' enemies, who placed a religious holiness tradition and practice as the top priority in life, Jesus was a dangerous heretic who threatened the authentic faith and life of the Jewish community. A whole way of life was at stake; a whole religious structure that guaranteed the tradition was endangered. The enemies of Jesus decided he had to die! Liberating people from disease and demons made Jesus a major publicity event in first-century Judea. Liberating them from the shackles of traditional religious authoritarianism with its dehumanization of life nailed Jesus to the cross outside the gates of the Holy City.

4. The Vulnerability of the Messianic Mission

The biblical faith portrays Jesus' life and mission as conflict and combat between the arrival of God's messianic kingdom and the powers of satanic evil. It sees those powers embodied in Jesus and in Jesus' adversaries. Jesus is portrayed in combat: in debate with antagonists, healing the sick and casting out the enemy powers from the possessed, raising life out from the realm of death. However, within this struggle Jesus refuses to participate in a violent, revolutionary battle on behalf of political freedom, justice and righteousness. Jesus' prophetic ministry ended in seeming defeat on a cross. Life within God's kingdom is thereby defined as combat not by might but by the spirit of love, which willingly is vulnerable unto death. Jesus certainly awakened hopes of a revolutionary struggle for justice and peace within the crowds and his disciples. John Dominic Crossan in *The Historical Jesus* devotes two excellent chapters to describing the militant, revolutionary context in which Jesus lived.[89]

The New Testament gives only glimpses of this possibility. John reports that after the feeding of the 5,000, Jesus withdrew because he knew that they wished by force to make him king (Jn 6:15); the Gospels report that one of his disciples, Simon the Zealot, was called from the ranks of the militant revolutionaries (Lk 6:16); the passion narratives report that Peter attempted to defend Jesus with a sword as Jesus was being betrayed by Judas Iscariot. Luke reports a question asked of Jesus by the disciples: "Lord, should we [plural] strike with a sword?" (Lk 22:49). John Howard Yoder believes that the second temptation of Jesus in the wilderness (Luke's order, Lk 4:5-8) was Satan's offer of "all the kingdoms of the world" through military conquest ("if you bow the knee before me").[90]

Within a revolutionary situation with its calls to militant insurrection, Jesus insisted on a nonmilitant struggle. Jesus denounced the rich and powerful, whether Roman or Jewish, for their oppressive and destructive relationships with the poor (Lk 6:20-26); however, Jesus refused to rally the hate and the vengeance of the poor and oppressed. In contrast, Jesus said, "But I say to you that listen, love your enemies, do good to those who hate you, bless those who curse you, pray for those who abuse you" (Lk 6:27-28). Note in particular when Jesus speaks to the Roman laws of occupation, which required Jewish civilians to carry the army pack of

---

[89]John Dominic Crossan, *The Historical Jesus: The Life of a Mediterranean Jewish Peasant* (San Francisco: HarperCollins, 1991). See Chapters 9 and 10.

[90]John H. Yoder, *The Politics of Jesus: Vicit Agnus Noster* (Grand Rapids: Eerdmans Publishing, 1972), 32.

Roman soldiers for a mile. "If anyone forces you to go one mile, go also the second mile" (Mt 5:41). It is probable that Jesus' refusal to accept the leadership of a people's revolution on Palm Sunday (Luke 19) is the reason that many of those who welcomed him to Jerusalem also called for his crucifixion and the release of a jailed criminal, Barabbas (Mt 27:15-26).

God limits God's messianic, transforming power within history to insistent and persistent love. That means God's messianic kingdom is vulnerable among us. Divine vulnerability means humanity can always say no to God's call to participate in God's messianic future. God's ultimate intentions can continually be frustrated. Furthermore, it means that God within history has chosen not to call on any authoritarian forces to protect or enforce God's ultimate will within life. God allows God's messianic cause, God's program or project, to be frustrated—even seemingly crushed. Jesus was hung in the terrifying darkness of Holy Friday, and heaven remained in apparent silence. Faith alone had the privilege of witnessing eternity's affirmation of Jesus crucified. Only faith sees the resurrected one and hopes within history's tragedies that the vulnerable God is the God to whom the future of humanity and the cosmos belongs!

The God manifest in Jesus crucified has nothing in common with numerous portraits of God created within our culture. The God of Jesus cannot be identified with the God who blesses the United States or any nation's security or military power. The God of Jesus has nothing in common with any God who promises financial reward, physical comfort, or a life without struggle for God's people. The God of Jesus challenges, critiques, and judges all forms of power and imperialism—cultural, economic, racial, or political. In contrast to the demons and divinities of invincibility worshiped and celebrated by American culture, the God of Jesus is essentially marked by vulnerability, by an infinite capacity to share and bear the cumulative weight of human pain and suffering. This is God incarnate in Jesus crucified and risen, the Cosmic Crucified. This is the God who takes the form of outstretched, open, spike-pierced hands, the God who is embodied in a half-naked human figure washing fishermen's feet, the God who like a mother hen scurries about clucking, gathering chicks under her wings in order to absorb the threat of death in her own body, the God who like a mother in childbirth gasps and cries to bring forth a new creation.

One of the most essential things that Jesus' cross says about God is that God does not meet humanity's common expectations. God is the ultimate source of light and life, the ultimate power behind the wind, the waves, and nuclear energy. God is often defined as the omnipotent (all-powerful) and the omniscient (all-knowing). Humanity has normally assumed that when the omnipotent appears, it will be perfectly obvious that God is here. One assumes that evil should crumble and mercy and justice prevail. Millions still argue that Jesus could not possibly be God's Messiah or Anointed Ruler because evil still flourishes.

If Jesus crucified is the Promised of God, then God manifests Godself in paradoxical form. God is revealed as the God who wills not to be "God." God manifests Godself in that which appears to be weakness, foolishness, lowliness. Paul writes, "we proclaim Christ crucified, a stumbling block to Jews and foolishness to Gentiles" (1 Cor 1:23). Christians have also described God as the one who appears to be hidden or concealed among us. In reality God is not hidden, but revealed in Jesus. God appears to be hidden only from the perspective of our expectations. God as the Cosmic Crucified is revealed as the one we did not expect.

Jesus' ministry was marked by the unexpected. Jesus said, "The kingdom of heaven is like treasure hidden in a field" (Mt 13:44), like leaven hidden in three measures of flour (Mt 13:33), like a tiny mustard seed hidden in the ground (Mt 13:31). Even John the Baptist, who had recognized the Messiah's arrival in Jesus (Mt 3:11-17), had serious questions about the nature of Jesus' ministry. It certainly did not appear "God-like" in John's eyes. He had expected more powerful signs and activities of a vice-regent of God (see Mt 3:11-17). John sent messages to Jesus saying, "Are you he who is to come, or shall we look for another?" (Mt 11:3). Jesus replied, "Go and tell John what you hear and see: the blind receive their sight . . . and blessed is he who takes no offense at me" (Mt 11:4-6).

Jesus knew that God's kingdom was present but certainly not obvious. One could stumble if one did not have eyes to see and ears to hear, because God was present in unexpected, surprising, and paradoxical form. God was hidden as the one who chooses not to be "God." Jesus crucified crystallizes and ultimately concretizes that dimension of our faith. If God is the God who allows God's Son to cry into heaven's seeming silence, "My God, my God, why have you forsaken me," then God certainly is hidden in the cross. Martin Luther in the Heidelberg Disputation writes, "For this reason true theology and recognition of God are in the crucified Christ."[91]

However, if it is true that the God who chooses not to be God is truly God, then no hell nor power can separate us from the love of God in Christ Jesus our Lord (Rom 8:38-39). When human experience seems to indicate the absence of God, when suffering and pain are met by the

---

[91]Timothy F. Lull, ed., *Martin Luther's Basic Theological Writings* (Minneapolis: Fortress Press, 1989), 30.

silence of eternity, then either God is not here or God is present but hidden within the suffering of human existence. The gospel of the Cosmic Crucified Jesus claims that God is present, though seemingly hidden, even in the depths of the most tragic suffering and death. The crucified Jesus was raised from the dead. God's promise is that no matter how deep one descends into the hell of human existence, God is still there: There is nothing that can separate us from the [hidden] love of God in Christ Jesus our Lord (Romans 8).

God lets himself be pushed out of the world onto the cross. He is weak and powerless in the world, and that is precisely the way, the only way, in which he is with us and helps us. Matthew 8:17 ("This was to fulfill what had been spoken through the prophet Isaiah, 'He took our infirmities and bore our diseases.'") makes it quite clear that Christ helps us, not by virtue of his omnipotence, but by his weakness and suffering."[92]

---

[92]Dietrich Bonhoeffer, *Letters and Papers from Prison* (London: Collins-S.C.M. Press, 1953), 122, (New York: Macmillan Publishing, 1971, new enlarged edition), 360-361.

3

THE WAY OF THE CROSS: THE COSMIC CRUCIFIED AND COSTLY MISSIONARY DISCIPLESHIP

The Christian community is brought into existence by God incarnate in Jesus Christ the Cosmic Crucified. It is God, that one who creates and permeates a universe of billions of galaxies, that one who in poetic terms throws stars across the heavens, who incredibly and passionately enters human existence and serves, suffers, agonizes, and is vulnerable unto death. That costly love is the forgiveness of our sins and the possibility of our life in communion with God. God in the Cosmic Crucified also entered into combat here on behalf of new messianic life in the arriving kingdom of God. The lost/damned are found; the poor are given hope; the sick are healed; the rich, powerful and religiously complacent are challenged. This messianic combat is waged with the power of vulnerable love, seemingly defeated but ultimately victorious as the crucified is raised and sits at the right hand of God. Now sin, Satan and death are conquered. The crucified is Christus Victor. God in Christ struggles for life, suffers unto death, and is raised that the cosmos might have life. That is the heart of our mission message.

Because this is the heart of it all, there is often a hesitancy within the Christian community to affirm that the church as the body of Christ in mission is also called to participate in God's struggle and God's suffering, as well as participating in Christ's gifts of forgiveness and resurrection. That, however, is a reality that permeates the biblical witness. A mark of the church is that while it lives within the victory over sin, death and the devil, it is called to costly missionary discipleship to be a serving, sacrificing, suffering church in order that the gospel of the Cosmic Crucified might encircle the globe and permeate every dimension of human life and history. This chapter explores the significance of this missiology of the cross for the life-style of the bearer of the gospel who proclaims the lordship of the crucified Jesus. The chapter begins by describing Christian discipleship in mission as being conformed to the Cosmic Crucified. Both the New Testament and the Lutheran tradition are used to show the legitimacy, relevance and power of a missionary form of life that is conformed to Christ.

This chapter explores discipleship as conformity with God incarnate in Christ in the light of the three dimensions of the cross of Christ described in the previous chapter. This missiology of the cross makes it impossible for the Christian community to separate the mission message from mission deeds. The question is not debatable, as it was in Jesus' message and in his life!

1. Discipleship in mission as God's call to passionate involvement in human brokenness and suffering (the second dimension noted chapter 2, D).
2. Discipleship in mission as God's call to participate in the messianic struggle for life in the midst of death (the third dimension noted in chapter 2, E).
3. Discipleship as God's call to vulnerability in mission (the first dimension noted in chapter 2, D).

A. Discipleship in Mission as Conformity to the Cosmic Crucified

One of the most powerful ways that the New Testament speaks of Jesus' call to missionary discipleship is to call the Christian community to conformity with the being and mission of God as it is incarnate in the being and the mission of the Cosmic Crucified. Walter Altmann writes, "We are free from the necessity to imitate Christ [the impossibility of Christian perfectionism] because his work is fundamental, unrepeatable and complete. But for the same reason we are free [from concern to establish our relationship to God] for new liberating actions [participation in messianic kingdom activities], in *conformation with the cross of Christ* and in accordance with what our imagination and discernment show us to be works of love" (emphasis added).[93]

Discipleship in mission is life in conformation with the cross of Christ. Jesus calls his disciples to take up their cross and follow him (Mk 8:35ff). Jesus promises that the disciples as bearers of the Good News to all nations (Mk 13:10) will be hated and persecuted because of bearing Jesus' name (Mk 13:9-13). Furthermore, in persecution they are blessed by God. "Rejoice and be glad, for your reward is great in heaven, for in the same way they persecuted the prophets who were before you" (Mt 5:11-12).

---

[93]Altmann, *Luther and Liberation: A Latin American Perspective*, 24-25.

In Philippians, Paul asserts that he desires, within the mission of the body of Christ, to share in Christ's sufferings (Phil 3:10ff). In 2 Corinthians he writes: "For while we live, we are always being given up to death for Jesus' sake, so that the life of Jesus may be made visible in our mortal flesh" (2 Cor 4:11). In sharing in Christ's sufferings, Paul believes that "I am completing what is lacking in Christ's afflictions [the continuing suffering-with-us God] for the sake of his body, that is, the church" (Col 1:24). Paul states that participation in the suffering of Christ is an introduction to being glorified with Christ (Rom 8:17). Similar themes are found in 1 Peter 2:18-25 and 2 Timothy 2:12-13. In addressing a persecuted and suffering church, Peter wrote, "For to this you have been called, because Christ also suffered for you, leaving you an example, so that you should follow in his steps" (1 Pt 2:21). Conformity with the Cosmic Crucified is costly suffering discipleship that is blessed by God and the privileged possibility of present joy and future glory.

The biblical witness broadens "conformity with the cross" to the whole life of Jesus beginning with the Cosmic Christ's condescension in the incarnation and including Christ's forgiving, self-giving love and humble servanthood. Paul calls the Philippian Christians to be conformed to the mind of Christ:

> Let the same mind be in you that was in Christ Jesus, who though he was in the form of God, did not regard equality with God as something to be exploited, but emptied himself, taking the form of a slave . . . and became obedient to the point of death—even death on a cross. (Phil 2:5-11)

The life and mission of the body of Christ is called to a discipleship conformed to this God-formed and cruciform ministry of humble servanthood that participates in God's vulnerability even to death.

The biblical tradition is rich in servant images, calling and mandating mission in conformity with the Cosmic Crucified. In John, Jesus says, "So if I, your Lord and Teacher, have washed your feet, you also ought to wash one another's feet" (Jn 13:14). Paul, in calling for generosity for the saints in Jerusalem asserts, "For you know the generous act of our Lord Jesus Christ, that though he was rich, yet for your sakes he became poor, so that by his poverty you might become rich" (2 Cor 8:9). In Galatians, Paul writes, "Bear one another's burdens, and in this way you will fulfill the law [the way] of Christ" (Gal 6:2).

All of these calls to be conformed with the Cosmic Crucified are ultimately calls to be conformed to the love of God revealed and incarnate in Jesus Christ. Love one another as I have loved you (Jn 13:34, 15:12). "We know love by this, that he laid down his life for us—and we ought to lay down our lives for one another" (1 Jn 3:16, 4:7-10). This love conformed to Jesus Christ forgives unconditionally (Col 3:13) and loves indiscriminately as God does—even unto the enemy (Mt 5:43-48; Lk 6:32-36). John Howard Yoder in *The Politics of Jesus* has provided an excellent discussion of Christian discipleship as being conformed to Christ in a chapter entitled "The Disciple of Christ and the Way of Jesus."[94]

As noted earlier, Altmann believes that the Lutheran tradition has forgotten "the necessity of following Jesus Christ in his path, of joining Jesus Christ in his kenosis, his emptying out."[95] Many Lutherans are concerned that calls to discipleship might be just one more sinful human attempt to justify oneself in the presence of God. This is particularly true if discipleship is understood as a form of humanly attainable sanctification—a process whereby one makes progress in a life of holiness.[96]

Discipleship, as God's call to conformity to Jesus Christ, has nothing to do with "attaining sanctification" or "self-justification." It is discipleship that experiences being overwhelmed by the awesomeness of God's self-giving, unconditional, costly love, that hears with joy Christ's promise of forgiveness, and rejoices in the privilege that the Cosmic Crucified makes possible in the call, "Come, follow me!"

Authentic discipleship recognizes that there is a tragic gap between the call to conformity with Jesus Christ as God's kingdom way in the world and one's own stumbling efforts to follow in the way of Christ. Therefore, Paul's declaration in Romans 6:1-4 that in Baptism we have died to sin is recognized by Luther in the Small Catechism as a daily drowning of the "old" sinful person in order that the "new" person conformed to Jesus Christ might daily arise to "walk in newness of life."

What does such baptizing with water signify?

---

[94]Yoder, *The Politics of Jesus*, 115ff.

[95]Altmann, *Luther and Liberation: A Latin American Perspective*, 24-25.

[96]For a discussion relating to this concern in contemporary Lutheran circles, see the 1987 Winter issue of *Word and World* entitled "Justification and Justice." Twenty-nine theologians from all of the Americas debated concerning the relationship between the gospel and discipleship committed to justice.

Answer: It signifies that the old Adam in us, together with all sins and evil lusts, should be drowned by daily sorrow and repentance and be put to death, and that the new man should come forth daily and rise up, cleansed and righteous, to live forever in God's presence.[97]

Martin Luther's famous document *The Freedom of a Christian* spells out the relationship between gospel and cruciform discipleship in two seeming paradoxical propositions:

1.   A Christian is a perfectly free lord of all, subject to none.
2.   A Christian is a perfectly dutiful servant of all, subject to all.

Under the first proposition, Luther states that ultimately and solely the Christian's life and future with God is an absolute unconditional gift of God in Jesus Christ. "One thing, and only one thing, is necessary for Christian life, righteousness, and freedom. That one thing is the most holy Word of God, the gospel of Christ."[98] Good works cannot contribute anything to this gift, but, on the contrary, they may be injurious if the Christian believes that one is justified by them.[99]

Luther then turns to the second proposition that the Christian is a "perfectly dutiful servant of all, subject to all." That is conformity to the servanthood of Christ. Luther can even speak of being Christ to the neighbor.

In describing this servanthood, Luther recognizes a continual struggle between the old and the new. The new person in Christ is obedient to God "out of spontaneous love in obedience to God and considers nothing except the approval of God, whom he would most scrupulously obey in all things."[100] However, this new person must struggle with the old within, which is not necessarily willing to die. Therefore, there is the daily dying and rising to be in conformity with the Cosmic Crucified. "So the Christian who is consecrated by his faith does good works, but the works do not make him holier or more Christian, for that is the work of faith alone

---

[97]Small Catechism in *The Book of Concord*, 349.

[98]Lull, *Martin Luther's Basic Theological Writings*, 597.

[99]Lull, *Martin Luther's Basic Theological Writings*, 610.

[100]Lull, *Martin Luther's Basic Theological Writings*, 611.

[trusting receptivity to God's unconditional costly grace]."[101] It is this faith which is active in love (Gal 5:6) and is called to conformity with Christ's servanthood. Luther writes in *The Freedom of the Christian*:

> Although the Christian is thus free from all works, he ought in this liberty to empty himself, take upon himself the form of a servant, be made in the likeness of men, be found in human form, and to serve, help, and in every way deal with his neighbor as he sees that God through Christ has dealt and still deals with him. This he should do freely, having regard for nothing but divine approval.[102]

> Hence, as our heavenly Father has in Christ freely come to our aid, we also ought freely to help our neighbor through our body and its works, and each one should become as it were a Christ to the other that we may be Christs to one another and Christ may be the same in all, that is, that we may be truly Christians.[103]

Gerhard Forde writing in *Christian Dogmatics*, Volume 2, concludes his discussion of the Christian life with these striking words:

> The Christian vision leads into the world, to suffering for and with others in the expectation of God's will being done on earth as it is in heaven. The aim is not to gain one's own holiness or to bring in the kingdom by force or tyranny, but to care for God's creatures and God's creation. "The creation waits with eager longing for the revealing of the sons of God." (Rom 8:19)[104]

One of the most powerful statements about cruciform life and mission is found in Dietrich Bonhoeffer's *Letters and Papers From Prison*:

> To be a Christian does not mean to be religious in a particular way, to cultivate some particular form of asceticism (as a sinner, penitent

---

[101]Lull, *Martin Luther's Basic Theological Writings*, 612.

[102]Lull, *Martin Luther's Basic Theological Writings*, 618.

[103]Lull, *Martin Luther's Basic Theological Writings*, 619-620.

[104]Gerhard Forde, "Eleventh Locus, Christian Life, Justification Today," in *Christian Dogmatics*, vol. 2, ed. by Carl Braaten and Robert Jenson (Philadelphia: Fortress Press, 1984), 468.

or a saint), but to be a man. It is not some religious act which makes a Christian what he is, but participation in the suffering of God in the life of the world.[105]

The biblical tradition as well as the Lutheran tradition, compels us to rethink both: 1) the cruciform nature of the gospel of the Cosmic Crucified; and 2) the cruciform nature of the ministry of those participating in the mission of God incarnate in the Cosmic Crucified. One must ask in the words of Walter Altmann why the Lutheran church in particular has forgotten "the necessity of following Jesus Christ in his path, of joining Jesus Christ in his kenosis, his emptying out."[106]

In the following sections, several implications for "missionary discipleship conformed to the Cosmic Crucified" are outlined. Each section on discipleship in mission relates to a previous section describing the mission of God incarnate in the Cosmic Crucified.

B. Discipleship in Mission and God's Call to Passionate Involvement in Human Suffering

The continuing suffering-with-us-God incarnate in Jesus has radical implications for the church's mission (chapter 2, D). If solidarity with human brokenness and pain defines one dimension of God's mission, then being conformed to Jesus Christ and participation in the mission of God will mean sharing in the brokenness and pain of the human community. In the thoughts of Matthew 25 and Exodus 3, there are afflictions to be seen, cries to be heard, and sufferings to be known. Discipleship is being captured by God in Jesus Christ, who moves into our lives, turning us inside out and upside down in order that we might with the Cosmic Crucified be swept into the world to share the depths of human pain and brokenness. "As the Father has sent me, so I send you" (Jn 20:21).

The mission of the body of Christ is marked by participation in human lives rather than indifference to and distance from human lives. Participation rather than indifference and distance is to mark every dimension of the life and mission of discipleship. In recent years, Christian ministry in the U.S.A. has been marked by a deep concern for counseling. Prophetic spokespersons in the field of pastoral counseling have called the

---

[105]Bonhoeffer, *Letters and Papers from Prison*, 1953 edition, 123.

[106]Altman, *Luther and Liberation: A Latin American Perspective*, 24-25.

church into the depths of human suffering. Behind the masks of social convention human lives are lived out in isolation, irresponsibility, guilt and failure as well as other forms of pain. If the mission of the body of Christ is to be conformed to Jesus Christ, it will follow Jesus into the inner depths of human existence. Within every human life there are afflictions to be seen, cries to be heard and suffering to be known. Good parents know this in their children; caring spouses know it in their loved ones; disciples of Christ are called to know it in each other and in the lives of those met in the world. The suffering-with-us God calls the Christian community into the depths of human lives—to be a suffering-with-us people.

The world is marked not only by inner pain but also incredible physical suffering, both corporate and individual. Statistics are so overwhelming that they become seemingly irrelevant to our daily lives. Nine hundred million persons malnourished, 40,000 children dying daily from inadequate diets and health care, 16 million refugees, 40 million Africans at the edge of existence because of recent drought, over 2 billion people without adequate water. Millions of those people live within Muslim and Buddhist communities. Thirteen countries with Muslim majorities of over 75% (seven with majorities over 90%) and with a total population of 500 million people have an average annual per capita income of less than $500 (1990 *Encyclopedia Britannica*). The lives of most of those millions are lived out beyond the horizons of our consciousness. However, the Cosmic Christ shatters the parochialness of our lives and calls us into solidarity with the world's suffering. There are afflictions to be seen, cries to be heard and suffering to be known.

Authentic Christian witness to the good news of the Cosmic Crucified takes place as disciples participate in the pain of the world. Within the pain (in contrast to distance) and in solidarity with suffering (in contrast to indifference) the Christian community proclaims in word and deed the saving power of the gospel.

The Lutheran community, as noted by Walter Altmann, has often neglected the call of God to the cruciform mission of the body of Christ—that is, the mission conformed to the Cosmic Crucified. We often have not heard the radical call of the Cosmic Crucified to discipleship, to follow Jesus into the depths of human existence. Recognizing this fact, the ELCA in its DGM statement of *Commitments for Mission in the 1990s* states:

We are committed to witness to Jesus Christ in both word and deed. We will preach the gospel and in Jesus' name we will seek to alleviate suffering and empower the weak and advocate for righteousness, justice and peace. We will work with the entire global community for justice, peace and the renewal of all creation. (Commitment 6)

C. Discipleship in Mission and God's Call to Participate in the Messianic Struggle for Life in the Midst of Death

The messianic cosmic struggle still permeates human life and history (chapter 2, E). The coming kingdom of God inaugurated in Jesus and for which we continue to pray ("Your kingdom come; your will be done on earth as in heaven") continues to be engaged in struggle with the demonic powers of darkness. As in Jesus' day, religious traditions dead to the living God continue to enslave human lives; the poor and oppressed continue to be exploited by the world's rich and powerful; the weak and diseased, like Lazarus at the rich man's door, are often neglected and relegated to the periphery of life, where their presence will not disturb.

Contemporary missionary discipleship is openness to God's call to participation in the continuing messianic mission of the body of Christ. The powers of darkness are to be met, combat to be entered, demons overcome, battles lost and battles won. The cross indicates that more often than not compassion, self-giving love, and the vulnerability of servanthood will be dominated and even crushed by the powers of evil and destruction. However, the resurrection of the Cosmic Crucified is God's promise to the disciples of Jesus that ultimately the future belongs to the God of our Lord Jesus Christ. This hope, which transcends both optimism and pessimism, is the driving power of the mission of the body of Christ.

But thanks be to God, who gives us the victory through our Lord Jesus Christ. Therefore my beloved, be steadfast, immovable, always excelling in the work of the Lord, because you know that in the Lord your labor is not in vain. (1 Cor 15:57-58)

1. *The Continuing Prophetic Voice*

Discipleship within the messianic struggle is marked by the continuing prophetic voice of the body of Christ. It is the Spirit-empowered voice (Rom 12:6, 1 Cor 12:10) that witnesses to Jesus Christ (Mk 13:11, Acts 1:8)

and in Jesus' name challenges the values and norms; that is, the principalities and powers of the twentieth and twenty-first century. It is this
prophetic voice in words and actions that makes the body of Christ the salt
and light of the world. In Jesus' words, if this prophetic voice, which
speaks an alien word in the world, loses its saltiness, then it has lost its
value (Mt 5:13). Likewise, an alien word of light in a world of darkness
must be lifted up to give light to the whole house (Mt 5:14). The Cosmic
Crucified continually challenges the body of Christ to be about its alien
prophetic mission, challenging the powers of darkness.[107]

In the last century, Søren Kierkegaard, the Danish religious thinker,
made a devastating attack upon the church of Denmark because of its
inability to speak God's alien word of truth within Christendom, which had
lost God's truth and lived in its own darkness. Kierkegaard charged that
the church had lost its prophetic voice because they had lost their
conformity with the prophetic crucified Christ, who had spoken God's
prophetic alien truth and suffered death for it.

According to Kierkegaard, the Christ who said, "Follow me," was the
Christ in his humiliation, not the Christ in his glory. Thus, the Christian
must become contemporary with the Christ who was despised and hated
for speaking God's alien prophetic truth. Only after sharing in the
humiliation and suffering of Christ can the Christian share in his
exaltation.[108]

Wherever people and messianic life are crushed, wherever love is
absent, justice perverted, the good betrayed, religion distorted, and the
beautiful disgraced, there the alien prophetic voice of the Cosmic Crucified
must be enabled to speak. God's prophetic alien word must be heard,
Repent, for the kingdom of God is at hand. People are to be challenged
to repentance in Jesus' name. For the sake of their own life and for the
sake of the lives they ignore and destroy, they are called to repentance and
participation in the messianic kingdom. To those who repent, who allow
their lives to be turned around and upside down, the Cosmic Crucified
promises your sins are forgiven; go in peace. To the recipients of that
costly gift, the Cosmic Crucified says, take up your cross and follow me,
as aliens in a foreign land.

---

[107]Stanley Hauerwas and William H. Willimon in *Resident Aliens* (Nashville: Abingdon, 1989),
develop a Christian ethic around the theme that Christians live as aliens in contemporary culture.

[108]Søren Kierkegaard, *Training in Christianity*, translated with introductory notes by Walter
Lowrie (London: Oxford University Press, 1941), 40, 58, 173.

2. The Contemporary Damned and Marginalized

Every generation and century has its particular marginalized who are consigned to live outside the circle of the chosen and righteous. In Jesus' day, there were "sinners" whose lives were not lived in conformity with what Marcus Borg terms the politics of holiness. There were also other marginalized: the poor, the oppressed, women, and gentiles, whom Jesus, challenging his contemporaries, incorporated within the circle of the compassion of God.

Mission conformed to Jesus Christ continues to mean crossing boundaries that exclude in order that all may fully participate in the new creation of the inaugurated messianic reign. Those boundaries vary from one culture or nation to another. In India there are the Dalits who are consigned to live outside of the Hindu caste system; in Japan there are the Burakamin who traditionally carried out the "unclean" work of society; in Latin America there are the landless farmers who have been driven from the source of their existence; in the U.S.A., Europe and South Africa, there are racial groups whose skin color denies them full participation in the cultural and economic privileges of society. The list of marginalized local and global peoples is endless and presents the followers of Jesus with continual challenges to follow the Cosmic Crucified across all boundaries with the self-giving inclusive vulnerability of the mind of Christ.

One of the most critical and universal boundaries of the 20th century is the boundary between male and female. The Christian church confronts this boundary on every continent both in the world and in the church itself, as well as in Muslim, Buddhist, Hindu and other religious communities.

Human culture for thousands of years and yet today exploits women and limits the potential of women in participating within the mission of the body of Christ. It is tragic that a number of persons within our Lutheran tradition have not been faithful to Jesus Christ, who radically challenged the sexism of his day by teaching women, touching "unclean women," sharing with women companions who later stood faithfully at the cross, and making Mary the first witness to the resurrection. The early church molded by the ministry of Jesus was a radically new community in which there was not Jew nor Greek, free nor slave, male nor female.[109]

Discipleship to Jesus compels us into solidarity with women. One dimension of this solidarity is sensitivity to our God language. Sensitivity to God language is important in tapping the tremendous gifts of women for

---

[109]Elisabeth Schüssler Fiorenza, *In Memory of Her: A Feminist Theological Reconstruction of Christian Origins* (New York: Crossroad, 1984), 34.

the mission of Christ. As long as male language is the primary (almost sole) way of speaking of God, people will (and do) conclude that feminine descriptions of God are not appropriate or less adequate in addressing or describing God. This in turn will imply for many that male humans are superior to female humans, having more gifts and potential as participants in the life and mission of the body of Christ. From my own reading, personal counseling and conversations with both women and men, I know this to be true for countless women. I know many women who, like many persons of color, struggle to remain within the church in spite of the fact that the church's male and white cultural language for God, the male chauvinism of many clergy, and the male prejudices prevalent within the Christian and missionary community make that almost intolerable.

In order to affirm that all women in the church are full participants, I believe the church should be sensitive in its use of God language and it should be supporting women as they search the Scriptures for feminine descriptions of God (there are many).[110] Balancing our God language affirms the God-given value of women and empowers the church for witness in the world.

There is another and even more important reason for the use of feminine symbols for God in our particular culture so often marked by domination, arrogance, aggressiveness, militarism and violence. Those characteristics, which often mark our culture, even our churches and theological discussions, are very often designated as male characteristics. Therefore, in our culture to say "God he" implicitly portrays to many people and particularly women a God who is aggressive and domineering if not militant and violent. In contrast, a missiology of the cross states that God is ultimately known in Jesus the Cosmic Crucified, in self-giving love, sacrificial service and vulnerability. These characteristics in our culture are often designated as female. Therefore, "God she" may be needed in our culture to speak God's alien word of truth and to witness to God who is incarnate in Jesus and vulnerable to death. I believe that this may be what is most frightening, particularly to males in our church who may be more deeply formed by our culture than cruciformed by the Cosmic Crucified.

Struggling with this issue as disciples of Jesus may be one of the most important things we do as we engage with Muslims and Buddhists around the globe. It is the Cosmic Crucified who compels the Christian community of disciples to see beyond the present destructive cultural walls

---

[110]Virginia Ramey Mollenkott, *The Divine Feminine: The Biblical Imagery of God as Female* (New York: Crossroad, 1989).

and boundaries between male and female and to envision a new creation in which there is neither male or female. Such a vision challenges not only Christians but Muslims, Buddhists, and the world.

> We are committed to developing a global mission program in which persons of every ethnic background, both women and men, are called and empowered to participate fully in the mission of Jesus Christ. (Commitment 8 in *Commitments for Mission in the 1990s*)

3. The Messianic Mission: The Restoration of the Totality of Creation

Jesus' prophetic, messianic mission was rooted in Israel's faith in God, who created the cosmos and called Israel into a mission of salvation. God is the creator of the heavens and the earth. All of life is God's creative handiwork and is under God's providential care. Jesus saw lilies of the field clothed beautifully and birds of the air fed bountifully by the hands of God (Mt 6:25ff). This same God was at work in Israel's history and spoke through prophetic voices. As promised by the prophets, God was now doing a new thing within creation. God's kingdom/reign was approaching, and all that had been distorted and destroyed by human indifference and disobedience to God would be reclaimed and restored. Jesus sent a message to John saying that the promises of God's new creation envisioned by Isaiah (Is 29:18-19; 35:5-6; 61:1) were being fulfilled:

> The blind receive their sight, the lame walk, the lepers are cleansed, the deaf hear, the dead are raised and the poor have good news brought to them. (Mt 11:5; Lk 7:22)

Biblical thought does not dichotomize life between the physical and spiritual in terms of matter and mind. Rather, life is unified by the creative Word and Spirit of God. God speaks and the cosmos exists (Genesis 1). God breathes and matter lives (Genesis 1-2). The Holy Spirit empowers Jesus, and he proclaims repentance and the kingdom's coming, does good, and heals all those oppressed of the devil (Acts 10:34-38).

We have emphasized that the gospel is centered in the proclamation of what God has already done in the life, death and resurrection of the Cosmic Crucified. This message is borne and preached by those conformed to the messianic mission of Jesus Christ and rooted in the reality of God, who is creator of heaven and earth. Therefore, the mission of the body of Christ has always been and will always be a mission of word and deed that is passionately concerned about the whole person, the whole community, the restoration of the whole creation.

It is within this context that the church as body of Jesus Christ becomes deeply involved in the totality of human brokenness. The hungry are to be fed, and food is shipped to northern Ethiopia, southern Sudan, Somalia, Mozambique, where millions of lives are at the edge of starvation. The poor are enabled to develop their own resources so that they may feed themselves, their own families and communities. The oppressed are supported in order that the chains of racism may be broken and all humanity may be free. With and within it all, the gospel of the Cosmic Crucified is always preached in order that all, even the dying and destitute, may live within the incredible costly love and promised victory of God.

It is this struggle to restore the whole of creation that still often leads to contemporary clashes between the kingdom of God and the powers of darkness. Servants are not above their masters. The disciples of Jesus will also meet demonic opposition and be set on trial before priests and kings (Mk 13:9-13).

Churches of the twentieth century clearly have borne the marks of the crucified Jesus. To be baptized or to baptize has meant imprisonment in Nepal. In Nigeria churches have been burned. Churches speaking for human rights in Central and South America have paid an incredible bloody price for their faithful prophetic ministry. Christians who witnessed to the gospel in Eastern Europe forfeited their educational and vocational future. For centuries the Coptic Church of Egypt has lived under Islamic law and rule, which has always discriminated against the minority Christian presence and at times has actually persecuted the Christian community. The Coptic Church understands itself as a martyr church. Prophetic voices within our own land and our own churches have been ignored, attacked, or socially silenced. The mark of Jesus' cross placed upon the Christian community indicates the costly struggle between the kingdom of God and the realm of darkness. It indicates the Christian community's ongoing participation in this cosmic conflict.

In El Salvador a small Lutheran church struggles against incredible odds. Persecution, oppression, imprisonment, and death have been daily realities. Terror touches life. But within the pain there is faith, hope, and love. There is the joy of Christian worship where the risen Christ is announced as Lord and where grace is proclaimed as final. There is also love that goes to work in human rights offices, trauma centers, agricultural development, and orphanages. These, too, are glimpses of the messianic kingdom, promises of things to come (Eph 1:4-5). Tears will be wiped away, and the people of God will cry a final "Amen" (Revelation 21).

Carl Braaten in *The Apostolic Imperative* writes:

> The cross has all too often been cloistered within the Sunday piety
> of the church, rather than being the dynamic of the everyday soldiers
> of the cross fighting for justice within the economic, social, and
> political situations of life.

> Although there are other humanitarian groups at work to alleviate
> suffering and degradation, poverty and hunger, the church will want
> to be second to none in doing everything within its power to lift the
> burdens of the million who starve, the races that are humiliated the
> nations that are held captive, [and] the classes that are deprived of
> full equality, etc.[111]

Braaten goes on to say that the unique aspect of the church's
mission is evangelism, and because no one else will do that, the church
must make certain that it does.

It is the messianic restoration of the totality of creation which leads
to DGM's Commitment 6:

> We are committed to witness to Jesus Christ in both word and deed.
> We will preach the gospel and in Jesus' name we will seek to
> alleviate suffering and empower the weak and advocate for
> righteousness, justice and peace. We will work with the entire global
> community for justice, peace and the renewal of all creation.

D. Costly Discipleship and God's Call to
Vulnerability in Mission

God in Christ crucified limits God's messianic, transforming power
within history to the power of love which draws and persuades (chapter 2,
E,4). This assertion is rooted in what God has revealed in the messianic-
kingdom mission of the crucified and risen Jesus. Participation in the
mission of God's kingdom is participation in God's promised future, which
is already present in Jesus Christ.[112] That future of God present in the

---

[111]Braaten, *The Apostolic Imperative*, 75.

[112]For a discussion of mission as rooted in the presence of God's future in Christ, see: Carl
Braaten's, *The Flaming Center*, chapter 2, 39-63.

Cosmic Crucified appears as vulnerable within history. This means that God has not and will not call forth any authoritarian force to protect or enforce God's ultimate messianic mission within history.

> [My servant] will not cry or lift up his voice, or make it heard in the street; a bruised reed he will not break, and a dimly burning wick he will not quench; he will faithfully bring forth justice. (Is 42:2-3)

This is precisely how the New Testament portrays the mission of the crucified Jesus: prophetic words of grace, challenge and repentance; acts of healing of the sick and exorcism for the captives; banquets with the stigmatized and ostracized; and advocacy for the poor and marginalized. Divine, costly and vulnerable love are present like leaven in a loaf, seeds planted in the ground. The kingdom of God is present but not recognizable unless one has eyes to see and ears to hear.

Participation in the messianic mission of God that actualizes God's future must be conformed to this cruciform, vulnerable, self-giving love manifest in Jesus the Cosmic Crucified. "As the Father has sent me, so I send you" (Jn 20:19-23). Wesley Ariarajah stated that religious pluralism demands that Christian witness be given in the spirit of one who has truly experienced the humility, the vulnerability and the self-giving that are at the center of Christ's own witness.[113] This study of the biblical faith affirms that the Cosmic Crucified mandates that there is no other way in which any witness to God revealed in the Cosmic Crucified might authentically be given.

This assertion is rooted in the conviction of Jesus Christ's finality and the absolute normativeness of God's incarnation in the Cosmic Crucified. As persons grasped by the finality of Jesus Christ, we are told that there is no other way. "If any want to become my followers, let them deny themselves and take up their cross and follow me" (Mk 8:34).

However, in listening to Jesus we are immediately confronted by the absurdity and inadequacy of the church's participation in the cruciform mission of God. The history of the Christian church is replete with examples when the Christian community harassed non-Christians or cooperated with military and social-economic forces to crush the so-called pagan world. From Constantine, who in 312 B.C. placed the sign of the crucified on battle banners; to the Christian Crusades, which fought numerous battles with the Muslim world to retake the "holy city" for Christian worship; to Charlemagne and St. Olaf who baptized thousands at

---

[113]Ariarajah, *The Bible and People of Other Faiths*, 70.

the point of the sword; to Ferdinand and Isabella, who threw the Muslim Moors and Jews off the Spanish peninsula; to Columbus and his followers, who on behalf of Europe's leading royal family and the Roman Pope decimated peoples and cultures in the name of the Crucified; to British warships that opened up China's seaports to opium trade and Western missionaries; to twentieth century America where many Christians find it impossible to witness to Jesus Christ without grafting the Christian message to this nation's concerns about national security—there has existed an overwhelmingly strong element within the Christian community that has refused conformity with the Cosmic Crucified. It has preferred a theology of glory and a love affair with a triumphant Christendom.

In contrast, there has also been within the Christian community a multitude of Christian witnesses whose message and mission has been conformed to the Cosmic Crucified. They have called people to repentance and proclaimed the atoning suffering of God and the agonizing, saving death of the Cosmic Crucified. They have, like Jesus, walked humbly among nations, learning and listening to peoples of every clime and culture. They have healed the sick, made the blind to see and enabled the crippled to walk. They have fed the hungry, clothed the naked and visited the imprisoned. They have advocated for the poor and marginalized. They have done all of these motivated and empowered by God's self-giving, vulnerable, costly love, which has captured their lives by the power of the Holy Spirit. They have gone as participants in God's mission into unknown places and times armed only by the power of the Spirit of God, who has chosen to be vulnerable among us. In participating in the vulnerability of that mission, many have sacrificed their lives and in so doing have participated in Christ's vulnerability unto death. Christ's vulnerability as Lord is our vulnerability as the disciples of the Cosmic Crucified.

The biblical call to conformity with the vulnerability of the Cosmic Crucified raises powerful questions concerning Christian participation in the social and political structures of society. This discussion has particular relevance to our conversations with Muslims, who firmly believe that the power of political structures can or should be used to impose God's will upon the life of the state, and with Buddhists, who have a long tradition of pacifism and non-violence.

E. Costly Discipleship and Participation in the World of Social and Political Structures

Participation in the messianic mission of the kingdom of God calls for conformity with the self-giving vulnerability of the Cosmic Crucified. Any mission witness to Jesus Christ is molded by the suffering servanthood of Jesus. Does this biblical affirmation preclude Christian participation in political power that imposes by force law and order upon a society?

In earlier discussions concerning the missiological statements of the ELCA/DGM, questions have been raised as to the relationship between this model for mission and the Christian life in society. For example, does this model for mission imply a Christian pacificism for all of life as argued by John Yoder? He concludes his volume, *The Politics of Jesus*, with this statement:

> A social style characterized by the creation of a new community and the rejection of violence of any kind is the theme of the New Testament proclamation from beginning to end, from right to left. The cross of Christ is the model of Christian social efficacy, the power of God for those who believe.[114]

John Yoder reflects an ancient Christian tradition of nonviolence rooted in Jesus' own cruciform ministry. George Forell quotes the early Christian theologian Tertullian (d. 220 A.D.) who argued that Christians could not serve in the imperial army.

> In this context Tertullian addresses the question of Christian service in the military. His answer is eloquent and direct: "There is no agreement between the divine and the human sacrament (sacramentum was the military oath of allegiance), the standard of Christ and the standard of the devil, the camp of light and the camp of darkness. One soul cannot belong to two lords—God and Caesar." Noting that on the night of his betrayal Jesus admonished Peter not to defend him with a sword, Tertullian concludes, "The Lord . . ., in disarming Peter, unbelted every soldier!"[115]

---

[114]Yoder, *The Politics of Jesus*, 250.

[115]George Forell, *History of Christian Ethics*, vol 1 (Minneapolis: Augsburg Publishing, 1979), 58.

This pacifist position reemerged during the time of the Reformation in the nonviolent anabaptist movement of Menno Simons. John Yoder eloquently represents this tradition.

Following the rise of Constantine to imperial power, the Christian community became more and more identified with the Empire. Forell notes Canon II of the Council of Arles (314 A.D.) "that threatens excommunication to a Christian soldier who throws down his weapons even in times of peace."*116* After Constantine, there emerged a political philosophy and practice that often fused and confused the life and work of church and state in what has been designated Christendom.

Martin Luther in seeking reformation for the church struggled to clarify the roles and relationships between church and state within Christendom. He observed the Roman church functioning like a political institution and attempting to play a political and military role within the Empire. He also observed the Holy Roman Empire interfering and attempting to control the life of the church. As Luther worked to clarify the roles of each to understand the Christian's responsibilities in the world, he spoke of God acting in love through two kingdoms or two ways of reigning in the world.

On the one hand there was the kingdom of God's right hand. Through this reign, which is the power of the gospel, God calls to repentance, proclaims the gospel, and brings forth in the Christian community works of compassion for the neighbor. Complementing the kingdom of the right hand is the kingdom of God's left hand, the law. This work of God is necessary because of sin and rebellion in the world, which are destructive of human life and community. Through God's reign of law with the left hand, God in love holds evil in check and works toward justice. In this kingdom of the left hand, God uses the force of social-political structures, in particular, the "power of the sword."

Luther was convinced that if all persons were true Christians, there would be no need for political structures because all people would spontaneously love their neighbor and walk in the will of God (the Ten Commandments). This would create a society that would be directed for the best advantage for the community. However, this is not the case.

Because society is marked by sin, evil, and forces destructive of life, political structures using force are needed "to preserve peace, punish sin, and restrain the wicked."*117* The Christian "submits most willingly to the rule of the sword, pays his taxes, honors those in authority, serves, helps

---

116Forell, *History of Christian Ethics*, vol 1, 60.

117Lull, *Martin Luther's Basic Theological Writings, Temporal Authority*, 668.

and does all he can to assist the governing authority that it may continue to function and be held in honor and fear."*118* Furthermore, the Christian should participate in government in order "that the essential governmental authority may not be despised and become enfeebled or perish. For the world cannot and dare not dispense with it".*119* The Christian does this out of love for the sake of the neighbor and others.

Luther recognized that life was incredibly complex. Jesus had said, love your enemies, turn the other cheek, give away your coat, be willing to suffer personal injustice; and Luther believed Christians were called to do this in personal life. However, the Christian, according to love, should not accept injustice for the neighbor. Love may demand justice for the neighbor's sake.

This illustrates one aspect of Luther's two kingdom thought. God in love rules through the gospel in the hearts of people. The same God in love rules the human community through social and political structures for the well-being of the community. Christians participate in both of these activities of God. The two must always be seen in relationship and interacting.*120* In other words, Luther believed God to be extremely well coordinated and ambidextrous.

This Lutheran perspective has been severely criticized because there has been a tendency for Lutherans to say that the church takes responsibility for the gospel and the state takes responsibility for law and order. This has often resulted in the church silently acquiescing to political oppression and injustice.

Carl Braaten in *The Flaming Center* writes, "Our belief is that Lutherans must be willing to take the lead in criticizing this doctrine of two kingdoms, perhaps above all others, because the Lutheran record in applying it on the boundary of church and state stinks with the rotting flesh of human beings in jail and concentration camps."*121* Braaten goes on to a more dialectical treatment of this doctrine, saying yes and no to certain of its elements.*122*

---

[118]Lull, *Martin Luther's Basic Theological Writings*, 668.

[119]Lull, *Martin Luther's Basic Theological Writings*, 669.

[120]Lull, *Martin Luther's Basic Theological Works*, 670.

[121]Braaten, *The Flaming Center*, 58.

[122]Braaten, *The Flaming Center*, 58-62.

Walter Altmann argues that at his best Luther saw the need for the necessary relationship between the two kingdoms. Altmann recognizes that Luther appeared at times to be subservient to the political authorities, especially the German princes who became protectors and benefactors of the Protestant revolt against Rome. However, Altmann asserts that Luther was a harsh social critic of these powers and illustrates this through Luther's interpretation of Psalm 82:2-4. He writes:

> In his introduction Luther shows how the princes, after having been liberated from the pope's tutelage through the Reformation's proclamation of the gospel, now want to be liberated from the gospel itself in order to, in their turn, be the dominators and even put themselves above God. They want to shut the mouths of the preachers who criticize them, accusing the preachers of being "revolutionaries" and "agitators." But the gospel is revolutionary, and it is part of the preacher's task to denounce that which is evil.[123]

Altmann then summarizes Luther's prophetic message to the princes found in Psalm 82. Luther "distinguishes three tasks: first, to guarantee the free preaching of the gospel, precisely critical and prophetical preaching; second, to defend justice and the rights of the weak and abandoned; and finally, to guarantee the order, peace, and protection of the poor."[124]

Luther was a radical in international politics, advocating a German revolt against the powers of Rome and the Emperor. On the other hand, he proved to be a conservative medieval, advocate of law and order in local politics, advocating suppression of the revolting peasants by the princes of the land. Luther was particularly perturbed by the fact that the peasant revolt was being carried out in the name Jesus Christ.

Menno Simons and Martin Luther represent two basic approaches to living out the Christian life within society. Menno Simons believed that conformity to the Cosmic Christ means that the Christian may not participate in violent imposition of law or the will of God upon people and nations. Christ always calls Christians to transcend violence in their prophetic words and actions intended to establish and preserve justice and peace within the community.

---

[123]Walter Altmann, "Interpreting the Doctrine of the Two Kingdoms," *Word and World*, Winter 1987, 54-55.

[124]Altmann, "Interpreting the Doctrine of the Two Kingdoms," 55.

Luther, on the other hand, believed that God and the world of sin and evil required that God work through both gospel and law. God calls Christians to participate in a variety of ways in God's work in the world. Preaching of the gospel and works of charity or compassion, the work of God's right hand are always carried out within the context of the vulnerability of love. However, for Luther the preservation of justice for others and peace for the nation often require that love sacrifice vulnerability in order to be effective in preserving life within a suffering, broken world.

There is never a question as to how Jesus Christ is to be presented in a world that does not know Christ. There is no question as to how those who preach the Cosmic Crucified are to bear that message into a world of religious pluralism. The message is to be molded by the cross. The message is Jesus crucified, who is love vulnerable unto death and who is to be borne by Christian witnesses vulnerable until death. The message is to be in words and actions that proclaim and manifest the gracious unconditional love of God. The gospel will be preached, the hungry will be fed, the sick healed and justice advocated in Jesus name.

However, when the new Christian community emerges, the question is raised, "What is their responsibility within their own world?" Will their lives always be molded by love vulnerable to death, or does God call the Christian community to full participation in political structures that could not survive unless the invulnerability of force is applied? There have always been Christians who have insisted that those called by Christ are called to live in Christ's new future messianic age, which in Christ is already present within the old age dominated by conflict, rebellion and hate. They believe that Christians are called to live with and in Christ in vulnerability to death as signs and promises of God's promised future.

Other Christians, including most Lutherans, have argued that as we live between the times, we are in Christ called to participate in the future through gospel-life; however, the powers of the old and present age that threaten human existence must be limited and controlled in order to sustain human community. Christians therefore are paradoxically called to be signs of God's gospel promise and participants in God's work of the law, preserving life in the present age threatened by the evil of social chaos.[125]

There are other approaches to Christian responsibility in the world. Many Christians have been willing to simply use the power of the state or the militant power of social revolutionary groups to attempt to impose the

---

[125]Putting Luther's two kingdom thought into biblical kingdom of God terms; that is, "the present age" and "the new or coming age" can be of assistance. I thank Graydon Snyder of Chicago Theological Seminary for discussions which have been of assistance in this area.

kingdom of Christ on society. One thinks of the monarchs Constantine and St. Olaf as well as Müntzer and militant Christian Marxist revolutionaries. This continues to be a major discussion within the Christian community, and it is also a major discussion in the dialogue between major religious traditions. Islam is very straightforward in insisting that Allah wills that the Muslim community actively work to impose the law of Allah (*Sharia*) upon society.

I once spoke to a group of seminary students about Christian witness within the Muslim world. I had focused on the necessity of a ministry carried out in conformity to the Cosmic Crucified. During the discussion period a Nigerian professor asked how I thought the Christian community in Nigeria should respond in the midst of the recent tension and clashes between Muslims and Christians in northern Nigeria. He said our people are tired of being told "to turn the other cheek, because we have already done that more than once." He raises a crucial question about Christian responsibility in a nation which is approximately evenly divided between the two faiths and also constitutionally mandated to preserve religious plurality. Do Christians rally their military and political forces and launch a defense against Muslim militants? Do Christians molded by the Cosmic Crucified continue to witness in a love that is vulnerable to death? Do Christians call upon all responsible citizens to uphold the constitutional guarantees of religious freedom and actively participate in the military and police power that may or may not preserve those constitutional rights?

For the Nigerian Christian churches it is a crucial debate; and unless Nigeria is an exception to Christian history, Christians will come to a variety of conclusions. Some will advocate that disciples of the Cosmic Crucified should live out Christlike nonviolence and as such be signs of the future. They may struggle for human rights, but they will be militant pacificists. Others will call for Christian responsibility under constitutional law. That may mean active participation in politics, the police and the military. There will also be others who in the name of the Crucified will exploit the frustration and traditional ethnic rivalries present in Nigeria, harnessing the prejudice and hatred of centuries, in order to fight a war of vengeance for the sake of a future Christian majority state. I believe that one can think with "the mind of Christ" about the first two alternatives. The third is clearly a denial of the lordship of the Cosmic Crucified.

4
DIALOGUE AND WITNESS AMONG BUDDHISTS AND MUSLIMS

This discussion of dialogue and witness must be understood within the previous discussion concerning the Cosmic Crucified and the mission of the church. We began this discussion by noting Wesley Ariarajah's critique of past Christian attempts at dialogue and witness. Ariarajah asserted that these initiatives began with the Christian community making exclusive claims for Jesus Christ and—contrary to Jesus' own ministry of self-giving, unconditional, vulnerable love—resulted in Christian arrogance, intolerance and domineering attitudes.

The thesis of this book has been that the Christian community does make absolute affirmations concerning Jesus Christ. However, these affirmations center in the fact that it is the self-giving, unconditionally loving, vulnerable and crucified Jesus who sits at the right hand of God. The Christian community affirms that it is precisely the one who is vulnerable unto death who transcends cultural and historical relativity. We then have explored some of the implications of the Cosmic Crucified for the mission of the church—that is, what does it mean to follow the crucified Jesus who from God's right hand says, "But you will receive power when the Holy Spirit has come upon you; and you will be my witnesses in Jerusalem, in all Judea and Samaria, and to the ends of the earth" (Acts 1:8)? It is now necessary to look for the specific implications of this missiology of the cross for our mission of dialogue and witness.

A. Speaking the Gospel

First, the dialogue and witness of the body of Christ will center in an awe-filled oral account of God's incredibly costly and pain-filled entry into human life in order that all might be saved and come to the knowledge of the truth (1 Tm 2:4). In joy-filled wonder, the disciples of Jesus Christ will search the language and cultures of the cosmos in order to witness faithfully to the awesome miracle that on Calvary God was vulnerable unto death for all and each of us.

Christian participation in dialogue and witness begins within the context of this faith. One of the primary implications of this vision is that every person, whether Christian, Muslim or Buddhist, is unconditionally and passionately loved by that Ultimate Reality at the heart of the universe. Every person met within every engagement of dialogue and witness has cosmic value and infinite worth. One is called to value those of such worth by listening to them and caring about them.

B. Crucified Minds

Second, the dialogue and witness of the body of Christ will be conformed to the Cosmic Crucified. "Let the same mind be in you that was in Christ Jesus, who, though he was in the form of God, did not regard equality with God as something to be exploited, but emptied himself, taking the form of a slave, . . ." (Phil 2:5ff). In the words of Kosuke Koyama, the Christian witness moves into the world with crucified minds. Authentic witness to Jesus Christ is borne by joy-filled witnesses humbled by God's incredible and unconditional grace. These disciples are called by the crucified and empowered by the Spirit to be conformed to the self-giving, vulnerable love of God in their witness.

They will walk in the baptismal promise of grace through which God in Christ daily cleanses of all sin. Daily they will hear Jesus say, "Die to that which does not conform to me and rise to the cruciform mission of the Cosmic Crucified." "Take up your cross and follow me" (Mk 8:34).

Ariarajah is no doubt correct when he notes that the Christian witness has often been arrogant, intolerant and even worse. However, if nothing else, it is hoped that this study has shown that the true recognition of the lordship of Jesus crucified will lead to humble, self-giving, vulnerable servanthood rather than to the opposite. Most of us will recognize that the Christian community is the first to be called to repentance and renewal in the presence of the Cosmic Crucified. If our message and mission are not conformed to Jesus Christ, then we are in danger of replicating the mission of some of Jesus' contemporaries who, Jesus claimed, crossed sea and land to make a single convert only to make them children of hell like themselves (Mt 23:15).

C. Participants in Divine Compassion

Third, the dialogue and witness of the body of Christ is rooted in God's suffering-with-us love that is divine compassion. Dialogue and witness begin with the assumption that God is already present and in solidarity with Buddhists and Muslims and has already seen their affliction, heard their cries and knows their suffering. Dialogue and witness conformed to Jesus Christ is compelled to be a suffering-with-us dialogue and witness—a presence of solidarity with people, with their joys and sorrows, hopes and crushed dreams.

On January 19, 1992, Dr. Albert Glock, an ELCA missionary, was murdered near Birzeit University on the West Bank. Glock was a professor of archeology at Birzeit University. He had begun his career like most Western biblical archaeologists, exploring the ancient civilizations of the Middle East. However, he became aware of the fact that there was little concern for the last 500 years or 1,000 years when the land was inhabited by the Palestinian Arab peoples. He saw this history ignored as recent history was scraped away to plumb the culture of the ancient Middle East—the times of Abraham, Jeremiah, or the Maccabees. In that process, he saw one more attempt to deny a Palestinian people their own history and tradition. With that concern primary in his mind, he gave his life to enabling Palestinian people to discover through archeology their own place within the history of the nations. Glock and his wife Lois literally chose to be in solidarity with a suffering and exploited people, both Muslim and Christian. The suffering-with-us God had called Al and Lois to be participants in the suffering-with-us body of Christ. "If one member suffers, all suffer together with it" (1 Cor 12:26). All authentic dialogue and witness begins in solidarity with people in their joys and in their pain.

D. Participants in the Messianic Struggle

Fourth, dialogue and witness is rooted in God's messianic struggle with the powers of darkness that distort and destroy God's creation and God's creative intentions for life filled with compassion, justice and peace. Persons cruciformed by the Cosmic Crucified will be participants in this divine struggle for compassion, justice and peace.

Christians engaged with Muslim and Buddhist communities will encounter people who also struggle for compassion, justice and peace. Muslims believe that Allah wills that all creation surrender to the will of

Allah and therein find justice and peace. Buddhists understand their eight-fold path to *nirvana* as including a walk of compassion, justice and peace. In spite of these differing perspectives, Christians, Muslims and Buddhists have shared problems, struggles and dreams that necessitate shared strategies on behalf of life.

The contemporary tension in Nigeria between Muslims and Christians is a critical example of the need for shared strategies on behalf of life. In Nigeria, 100 million people live on the edge of a catastrophic war of mutual annihilation. It is mandatory that Christians participating in dialogue and witness seek with Muslims for solutions that will result in life not death.

E. Conversations in Behalf of a Common Life

Fifth, authentic interfaith dialogue or conversations must begin with mutual conversations between Christian and Buddhists or Christian and Muslims concerning the value and meaning of life; the brokenness and suffering as well as the joys of people; the common visions and struggles for compassion, justice and peace. As Christians, we are called to carry on those conversations within the call of the Cosmic Crucified to love and serve unconditionally all people regardless of nationality, race, or religious identity, even if it means someone designated "the enemy."

> "You have heard that it was said, 'You shall love your neighbor and hate your enemy.' But I say to you, Love your enemies and pray for those who persecute you, so that you may be children of your Father in heaven; for he makes his sun rise on the evil and on the good, and sends rain on the righteous and on the unrighteous. For if you love those who love you, what reward have you? Do not even the tax collectors do the same? And if you greet only your brothers and sisters, what more are you doing than others? Do not even the Gentiles do the same? Be perfect, therefore, as your heavenly Father is perfect." (Mt 5:43-48)

Interestingly, the Qur'an in Surah 5:48 reads:

> And to you [O Muhammad!] We have sent down the Book in truth as a confirmer of the Books [i.e., all Revelations] that have come before it and as a protector over them . . . For each one of you [Jews, Christians, Muslims], We have appointed a path and a way,

and if God had so willed, He would have made you but one
community but [He has not done so in order] that He try [all of]
you in what He has given you; *wherefore compete with one another
in good deeds.* . . . (emphasis added)[126]

Theological dialogue or Christian-Muslim conversations should take
place within these broader conversations and shared struggles for life.
Within this context, the possibility exists for mutual respect and mutual
understanding. Only as people live with and for each other can honest
conversations take place concerning one another's deepest religious
convictions, clarifying how each of us understands life and faith similarly
and/or differently.

F.   The Necessity of Witness and Dialogue for Muslims,
Buddhists and Christians

Within this context one can begin to discuss one of the more
controversial questions concerning the purpose of Christian mission among
Buddhists and Muslims. Is the purpose of Christian mission among
Buddhists and Muslims a dialogue through which clarity and mutual
enrichment can take place? Or is the purpose of mission grounded in the
hope that Buddhists and Muslims eventually might be grasped by God's
grace spoken and embodied in Jesus? This presentation argues that it will
be both.

1.   Necessary Witness

Christianity, Islam and Buddhism have been missionary in nature.
Although there are exceptions, members of these religious communities
have believed that they are called to give witness to the form of faith that
has grasped them. By their very nature these communities desire to share
what they believe to be the final word of truth to humanity. Gautama
Buddha chose to share the truth of liberation with his disciples, and
bodhisattvas, particularly within Mahayana Buddhism, renounce their crossing
to *nirvana* in order to share the truth of their journey with suffering
humanity. Muslims from the time of Muhammed have understood
themselves to be vice-regents of God who are called to bring Allah's will

---

[126]Fazlur Rahman, *Major Themes of the Qur'an* (Minneapolis: Bibliotheca Islamica, 1989), 144.

into every dimension of life. Jesus knew himself as sent from God to preach repentance and incorporation into the new life of the kingdom of God. In turn, the Cosmic Christ sends his disciples into the world: "As the Father has sent me, even so I send you" (Jn 20:21). When Buddhists, Muslims and Christians meet, our traditions call all of us to witness. If any of us denies this, we deny our existence as a people who believe that we are captured by final truth to be shared with suffering people.

2.   *Dialogue for Listening–Affirmation, Understanding and Enrichment*

Dialogue is first participation in God's self-giving and vulnerable love for people. Divine love always includes concern for the value and well-being of the one loved and necessarily affirms the other. Love affirms people, creating "somebodies" out of "nobodies."

One of the most powerful ways that love affirms people is by listening to them. Listening to a person values and respects the inner life and being of the other. Vulnerable love goes further and through listening is willing to receive and value the inner life of the other, even though it may sound strange and dissident. Dialogue in participation with the Cosmic Crucified necessitates listening love as affirmation and respect of someone created in the image of God and someone for whom God in Christ suffered and is suffering.

The possibility of witnessing, which all three traditions call for and desire, can take place only if Buddhists, Muslims and Christians actually understand each other. Authentic Christian witness among Buddhists depends on Buddhists actually hearing the biblical witness to Jesus. Authentic Muslim witness among Christians depends on Christians actually hearing the message of Muhammad. In order to understand another person's faith and effectively witness to Jesus crucified, it is essential to attempt to understand the faith of Muslims and Buddhists as they believe it should be understood.

There are innumerable barriers to this sharing of faith through witness. The centuries of separation and alienation demand that the Christian community take absolutely seriously the cruciform mission of the church within the Muslim and Buddhist world. Furthermore, the centuries of religious and theological misunderstanding demand that patient in-depth dialogue always be the context for witness to the faith.

Since persons of faith and rich religious traditions are found within Christian, Muslim and Buddhist communities, sincere and honest dialogue cannot be anything other than enriching. John B. Cobb, Jr. in his book *Beyond Dialog* states that dialogue between Buddhists and Christians has possibilities for mutual enrichment and what he calls mutual transformation as dialogue enables all participants to see their own vision from new and valuable perspectives.[127]

G. Implications of the Biblical Inclusive Theme
for Dialogue and Witness

Contemporary theology as articulated by Hick, Ariarajah and Knitter is marked by a universalism that challenges the nature of Christian witness among peoples of other faiths. As noted earlier, religious relativism assumes that God is universally present and God's revelation and/or saving power are universally present to the whole human community. Religious relativism also assumes that there are numerous revelations of God that reveal who God is and what God thinks and does. A third presupposition of religious relativism claims that all of these revelations are in some sense authentic, and none of them is the normative revelation by which all other revelatory claims are to be judged. The bottom line for this position is that Jesus is one among many revelatory events. The human challenge is to seek through Jesus and all these revelatory events for an understanding of the ultimate mystery within the universe. In Hindu terms, we are all on paths toward God's truth, and meaningful conversations will facilitate our common human journey.

We have not adopted that perspective; however, we have noted the importance of God's presence and revelation within every people and their culture. God is universally present to the whole of creation and to the whole human family. That is clearly a major biblical theme, manifest in God's creation and care of the whole universe (Genesis 1); God's universally present wisdom, which works within human personalities and structures (Proverbs 8; Romans 2); God's covenant through Noah with the entire human family (Genesis 9); God's call of Abraham and Israel for the blessing of all the nations of the earth (Genesis 12, Isaiah 42 and 49); God's planting of the human search for God within all people (Acts 17); and God's plan to recreate and restore all of creation (1 Cor 15:20-28; Eph 1:9-10; Phil 2:9-11). Within the biblical accounts this universal presence and wisdom of God is seen in concrete people outside the household of the biblical faith such as Melchizedek (Genesis 14), Jethro (Exodus 18),

---

[127]John B. Cobb, Jr., *Beyond Dialog: Toward a Mutual Transformation of Christianity and Buddhism* (Philadelphia: Fortress Press, 1982).

Ruth, Job, the Roman centurion (Mt 8:5-13), the Syrophoenician woman (Mk 7:24-30). Jesus pointed to the same universal reality in his parable of the Good Samaritan (Lk 10:25-37) and in his announcement that, "Many will come from east and west and sit at table with Abraham, Isaac, and Jacob in the kingdom of heaven, while the sons of the kingdom will be thrown into the outer darkness" (Mt 8:11-12).

This biblical theme is supported by the universal Christian experience that continually encounters persons of integrity and authentic openness to God's will and truth outside our own religious tradition. At times one finds persons who have understood the mission and message of Jesus with far greater depth than most Christians. M. K. Gandhi, the Indian advocate of nonviolence, is certainly one of those persons. Gandhi writes of Jesus:

> What then does Jesus mean to me? To me he was one of the greatest teachers humanity has ever had. To his believers, he was God's only begotten Son. Could the fact that I do or do not accept this belief make Jesus any more or less an influence in my life? Is all the grandeur of his teaching and doctrine to be forbidden to me? I cannot believe so. To me it implies a spiritual birth. My interpretation, in other words, is that in Jesus' own life is the key to the nearness of God: that he expressed as no other could the spirit and will of God. It is in this sense that I see him and recognize him as the Son of God.[128]

As Christians, we are called in our dialogue and witness to take this biblical affirmation of God's universal, cosmic presence and revelation seriously. We will always be looking for the footprints of God in people's lives. As we listen to people who are created in the image of God and who are bought with the price of the pain of God incarnate in the Cosmic Crucified, we will listen for insights into that which is good, beautiful and true—the will of God.

Recognition of sin as human brokenness and rebellion will prevent us from idealistic naivete that glosses over what is distorted in human lives, cultures and religions. However, in dialogue and witness, one is called to look for the best in other people's lives and faiths. One who believes that God's final truth is incarnate in the Cosmic Crucified will not find it necessary to berate another person's faith in order to make Jesus Christ "look good." The Christian rests in the trust that there is no past or future

---

[128]M. K. Gandhi, *What Jesus Means to Me*, compiled by R. K. Prabhu (Ahmedabad: Navajivan Publishing, 1959), 4.

revelation of God that will negate the hope in the Cosmic Crucified; namely, that at the heart of the universe is the God willing to go through death and hell for humanity's sake. This will always be the heart of our Christian witness.

5

THE UNIQUE THEOLOGICAL TASK OF ENGAGING WITH MUSLIM PEOPLES IN DIALOGUE AND WITNESS

In 1960 Daud Rahbar, a Muslim scholar, published a book entitled *God of Justice*.[129] In it, he argued that Allah as revealed in the Qur'an was not a *"capricious tyrant"* as some non-Muslims charged, but rather was the God of justice.[130] The book reflects a careful study of the Qur'an supporting this thesis. Fazlur Rahman makes a similar statement in his well-known book, *Major Themes of the Qur'an*, where he states "the ultimate reality . . . is conceived in Islam as *merciful justice* rather than fatherhood" (emphasis added) as in Christianity.[131] Christians need to note that it is indeed *merciful* justice advocated by Muslims like Rahman.

Later in his life Daud Rahbar became a follower of Jesus. He was asked why he had made that move. In his autobiography he replies to this question. In a short statement recounting why he had become a Christian, he comments that humanity searches for the "worshipable," and his autobiographical sketch portrays a Muslim in search of that which is worthy of worship and adoration.[132] As a Muslim, he had meditated upon the ultimate mystery and nature of Allah who was Allah *akbar*; that is, "God is greater," greater than any human conception. No predicate is adequate to describe the ultimate wonder of God. One thinks of Anselm's definition

---

[129]Daud Rahbar, *God of Justice: A Study in Ethical Doctrine of the Qur'an* (Leiden, The Netherlands: E. J. Brill, 1960).

[130]Rahbar, *God Justice*, xii.

[131]Rahman, *Major Themes of the Qur'an*, 29.

[132]Daud Rahbar, "Memories and Meanings" (Boston University, 1985, Photocopied), 359-360.

of God as that "than which nothing greater can be conceived."[133] Like every Muslim, Daud Rahbar had daily prayed with his forehead in the dust, surrendering himself to Allah (*Islam* literally meaning "to surrender") and in that surrender had sought significance and peace for life.

Rahbar then relates that in talking with Christian friends and reading the New Testament he was struck by the account of Jesus' self-giving love and his sacrificial death (Muslims do not accept the reality of Jesus' death). In this self-giving, suffering love, Rahbar says he encountered a most excellent love, "a love worthy of the eternal God." He was grasped by that love and concluded that this most excellent love must be of God. It is interesting to note that it is the heart of the gospel which grasped Daud Rahbar.

Fazlur Rahman, the outstanding Muslim scholar, however, sees Christianity's focus upon sacrificial love as a major weakness within the Christian faith. In contrast to Rahbar, he writes, "But such religious ideologies as have put their whole emphasis upon God's love and self-sacrifice for the sake of His children have done little service to the moral maturity of man."[134] Rahman asks when is man to become responsible for his own life, when is he to come of age?[135]

A. Costly Grace and Merciful Justice

After a talk in which I had told the story of Daud Rahbar, a Muslim, Amin, came up to me and said, "I don't think you interpreted Islam correctly because you did not explain that Muslims also believe in a merciful, forgiving God as well as a God of justice." I apologized to him and said that I would like to talk with him about his understanding of justice and mercy. After a lengthy discussion, we agreed that Muslims look

---

[133]*Saint Anselm, Basic Writings, Proslogium* trans. S. N. Deane, 2nd ed. (LaSalle, Illinois: Open Court Publishing, 1962), chapter 2.

[134]Rahman, *Major Themes of the Qur'an*, 9.

[135]It is interesting to note that it is exactly in Christ's weakness and suffering that Dietrich Bonhoeffer sees the possibility of humanity coming of age and taking responsibility for life in the world: "This is the decisive difference between Christianity and all religions. Man's religiosity makes him look in his distress to the power of God in the world; he uses God as a *Deus ex machina* [literally 'God out of a machine' from ancient dramas where Gods were let down from above to save someone in distress]. The Bible, however, directs him to the powerlessness and suffering of God; only a suffering God can help." A suffering God calls humanity to come of age taking responsibility for life. (From *Letters and Papers from Prison*, 122, 174.)

at mercy through the lens of justice, while Christians look at justice through the lens of mercy as costly grace. During a later session, Amin was asked to give his interpretation of Islam to the group.

After his presentation, he was asked whether Muslims believed that God would always forgive. He replied that he did not think that forgiveness in every case would be possible because justice might be violated. He thought that from the perspective of Islam, Allah would take into account every person's total life. Allah would certainly be mercifully forgiving; however, that forgiveness could not be unconditional. Forgiveness and mercy would be limited by God's concern for justice.

Fazlur Rahman, recognized as one of the most distinguished interpreters of Islam, speaks in similar terms. Interpreting the Qur'an, Rahman writes: "Several other verses also indicate that God will pardon or overlook men's lapses, provided the overall performance is good and beneficial."[136]

Surah 4:31 reads: "If you avoid the major evils that have been prohibited you, we shall obliterate occasional and smaller lapses"[137] Merciful justice is at the heart of Islam and is seen as the impetus for humanity's moral growth and maturity.[138]

In contrast to Islam's merciful justice, the Christian message centers in the costly unconditional love of God. At the time of his baptism, Daud Rahbar stated that "the paradox of God's mercy and justice troubled me and that I wanted to relate to God on terms of His unconditional mercy."[139] As Christians engage with persons of other faiths, they will find that the gospel is unique in proclaiming the costly suffering grace–vulnerability unto death–present in the Cosmic Crucified.

The outstanding Christian interpreter of Islam, Kenneth Cragg writes, "At the heart of 'the gospel of the blessed god,' is a proven divine capacity to love and the cross is where we can know it so. There too is a bearing of evil which is a bearing away of it. . . . It is an acknowledgment which Christian thought and experience find the more authentic as *awareness of other faiths makes its distinctiveness the more compelling*" (emphasis added).[140]

---

[136]Rahman, *Major Themes of the Qur'an*, 30.

[137]Rahman, *Major Themes of the Qur'an*, 30.

[138]Rahman, *Major Themes of the Qur'an*, 29-30.

[139]Rahbar, *Memories and Meanings*, 350.

[140]Kenneth Cragg, *The Christ and the Faiths* (Philadelphia: Westminster Press, 1986), 324.

While teaching in Nigeria in the 1960s, I met a Pakistani Muslim, Azmi, who became a good friend. He was a man of deep devotion, literally surrendering every detail of his life to the will of God. From his five daily prayers commanded by the Qur'an to the shape of his beard, which he found in the *hadith*, or the traditions concerning Muhammad, Azmi lived in conformity to the will of Allah. He was also a zealous witness to his faith, continually talking to his students and friends about the richness of the Islamic tradition.

One day as we shared dinner, he said, "You know I have a disturbing dream that recurs again and again. I am standing at the edge of an abyss. Allah awaits on the other side as my judge. The only way that I may cross is to walk on a narrow rope, and I am falling off." Does Allah wait in merciful justice energizing our moral responsibility in preparation for Allah's final judgment, as believed by Fazlur Rahman and my friend Azmi? Or does God in suffering, sacrificial love cross the abyss to us, entering our lives, bearing our sins and promising that our sin and failures can never separate us from the love of God in Christ Jesus?

Fazlur Rahman argues that the Christian focus upon costly grace leads to human irresponsibility. Christians will have to agree that this has often been the case since the times of the Apostle Paul, who wrote: "Should we continue in sin in order that grace may abound?" (Rom 6:1) "By no means!" replies Paul, because the disciples of the Cosmic Crucified are persons conformed to Christ—they are a cruciform people!

> Do you not know that all of us who have been baptized into Christ Jesus were baptized into his death? Therefore we have been buried with him by baptism into death, so that, just as Christ was raised from the dead by the glory of the father, so we too might walk in newness of life. (Rom 6:3-4)

Christians engaged with Muslims will repeatedly discuss this message of merciful justice and costly grace. It will be the occasion for difference, debate and for drawing some persons to the foot of the cross.

B. Incarnation and *Shirk*

The Qur'an's basic critique of Christianity is that it has elevated that which is human, Jesus, and has identified Jesus with God.

O People of the Book!
Commit no excesses
In your religion: nor say
Of Allah aught but the truth.
Christ Jesus the son of Mary
Was (no more than)
A Messenger of Allah.
And His Word,
Which He bestowed on Mary,
And a Spirit proceeding
From Him: so believe
In Allah and His Messengers.
Say not "Trinity:" desist:
It will be better for you:
For Allah is one God:
Glory be to Him:
(Far Exalted is He) above
Having a son. To Him
Belong all things in the heavens
And on the earth. And enough
Is Allah as a Disposer of affairs.[141]

Fazlur Rahman writes: "You may not point to any human being, with delimitations and a date of birth, and say simply, 'that person is God.' To the Qur'an, this is neither possible, nor intelligible, nor pardonable."[142] Rahman also states: "In any case, the unacceptability of Jesus' divinity and the Trinity to the Qur'an is incontrovertible."[143] For Islam there is an infinitude about the reality of God that no element of creation shares. "It is precisely this belief in such sharing [creaturehood participating in Godhood] that is categorically denied by the Qur'anic doctrine of *shirk* or 'participation in Godhead.'"[144]

---

[141]Surah 4:171, also 5:117; 5:72-75.

[142]Rahman, *Major Themes of the Qur'an*, 168.

[143]Rahman, *Major Themes of the Qur'an*, 170.

[144]Rahman, *Major Themes of the Qur'an*, 13.

It has often been noted that Muhammad probably encountered a form of Christianity that associated Jesus and Mary with God in a manner not acceptable to orthodox Christian teaching and that similar nonorthodox views continue within the Christian community today. No matter where that discussion leads, Islam does raise the question as to whether the Christian faith affirms, as it desires, monotheism. Is Christian conversation concerning the Trinity a unique manner of affirming the unity of God, or is it a deterioration of monotheism into tritheism? Christians would affirm the former; Muslims are convinced of the latter. This will necessarily be a major discussion whenever Muslims and Christians dialogue.

From the Christian perspective, three basic principles enable and impel the Christian community to speak of the incarnation and Trinity, and all three arise out of Christian convictions concerning God's revelation. First is the resurrection of Jesus from the dead. This event is God's declaration that God's will has been spoken and lived in the life of Jesus of Nazareth. In the words of Robert Jenson, quoted earlier, "Only the resurrection of the dead will verify Yahweh's self-introduction as God."[145]

There is a second principle that lies behind the Christian affirmation of the incarnation. The principle is the affirmation that God moves into history and human lives to reveal and speak God's word. The form of biblical revelation is strikingly different than the form of Qur'anic revelation. From a Muslim perspective, the Qur'an is Allah's Arabic verbal message given to Muhammad to be recited for God's people. Allah speaks; Muhammad recites. Some biblical prophetic passages are understood in this way. For example, "The word that came to Jeremiah from the Lord: Stand in the gate of the Lord's house, and proclaim there this word, and say, Hear the word of the Lord" (Jer 7:1-2).

The biblical message, however, takes many other forms, such as prayers and hymns from people's hearts, documented history, biographical accounts of prophets lives, letters and Gospels. Here God speaks within and through human lives and experiences. As God's word is communicated through the lives and history of a people, God is the suffering-with-us God, the God who, for example, is intimately wrapped up in the marriage of Hosea the prophet (Hosea 1-3) or the return from exile by the people of Judah (Isaiah 40ff). God speaks in Hosea's painful experience of an unfaithful wife and in the life of his suffering servant people and prophet. God's activity and speech are so intimately involved in the life of God's prophets and people that God's Word passes into the

[145]Jenson, *The Triune Identity*, 33.

very being of the prophet. Terence Fretheim writes, "In some sense God takes up 'residence' in the very life of the prophet. The prophet becomes a vehicle of divine immanence."[146]

Fretheim concludes his essay: "Finally, we should note that the prophet's life as embodied word of God is partial and broken. The OT does not finally come to the conclusion that God was incarnate in a human life in complete unbrokenness or in its entirety. The word of God enfleshed in an unbroken way in the totality of a human life must await a new day. Yet, in the prophet we see decisive continuities with what occurs in the Christ-event. God's act in Jesus Christ is the culmination of a long-standing relationship of God with the world that is more widespread in the OT than is commonly recognized."[147]

For the Christian community, Jesus the Cosmic Crucified is the incarnation of God, the suffering-with-us God. Here in this personality, the Word of God is fully expressed. Kenneth Cragg writes: "Whereas the ultimate speech of God for Islam is prophecy, 'sealed,' as the phrase goes, or accomplished, in Muhammad, the speech of God for the Christian is personality . . . the Person of Jesus Christ in the flesh."[148]

Willem A. Bijlefeld in his essay "Christian Witness in an Islamic Context" observes that in contrast to the Christian perspective outlined by Fretheim, Muslim thinkers have advocated that revelation is not intimately related to history; it is rather atemporal and ahistorical as God's Word from eternity strikes into the temporal. Any other form of revelation from a Muslim perspective compromises the nature of Allah. "The whole issue of 'God and history' would seem to be one of the major points for Christian-Muslim conversations and reflections."[149]

Kenneth Cragg suggests that Christians raise with Muslims the question as to whether one limits the sovereignty of God by prescribing what is possible for the reality of God:

---

[146]Terence Fretheim, "God and Prophet: An Old Testament Perspective," *God and Jesus: Theological Reflections for Christian-Muslim Dialog* (Collection of papers prepared by The American Lutheran Church's Board for World Mission and Inter-Church Cooperation Task Force on Christian Witness Among Muslims, Minneapolis, Minnesota, 1984-86, Photocopied), 38. See also Appendix 1 to this volume.

[147]Fretheim, *God and Jesus: Theological Reflections for Christian-Muslim Dialog*, 42.

[148]Kenneth Cragg, *The Call of the Minaret*, rev. ed. (Maryknoll, New York: Orbis, 1989), 244.

[149]Willem A. Bijlefeld, "Christian Witness in an Islamic Context," *God and Jesus: Theological Reflections for Christian Muslim Dialog*, 77. See note 146.

Must God not be left to determine the steps of the divine purpose and shall we say no? If so, then we can never say that the Incarnation could not be. If it cannot be denied as a possibility, then any claims of occurrence cannot be ruled out in advance. They must be investigated as a matter of historical evidence. Such investigation brings us back to Christ in human history.[150]

Third, the impelling principle that has driven the Christian community to speak of Christ as the incarnation of God is a response to the question as to whether God in revelation may be other than God who is the revealer. This was a question raised within the early church as it moved into the hellenistic culture of the Roman Empire. Within the early Aramaic-speaking church, it was possible to confess the finality of Jesus the Cosmic Crucified in messianic terms. Jesus as Messiah fulfilled all the promises of God that had been envisioned by the Old Testament prophets. The early church assumed that God, the ultimate reality, was present within Israel and by the power of the Holy Spirit was active for the restoration of all creation. The Spirit had inspired the prophets, created the Messiah in Mary's womb, empowered the messianic mission of Jesus, raised Jesus from the dead, and was poured out upon the early church. There was no question within the early church that when one encounters the Cosmic Crucified one encountered the reality and power of God. There was no question as to whether one met the revealer in the revelation, whether God ultimately might be other than God was in Jesus the crucified, risen and returning Messiah.

Within hellenistic culture it was otherwise. The world of spiritual being in the hellenistic world was hierarchical, and at the apex of that world of the divine was the ultimate—the One. This ultimate One was totally transcendent having no possibility of being related to lower realms of spirit, much less to the physical world of body and soul. The early Christian Arians taught that the Word of God incarnate in Jesus was a reality other than the Ultimate One. The *logos* that became incarnate was a second God created by and different from the Ultimate One.

They had views that Fazlur Rahman states would have been more acceptable to the Qur'an. Rahman writes, "The Qur'an would most probably have no objections to the Logos having become flesh if the Logos were not simply identified with God and the identification were understood less literally."[151]

---

[150]Cragg, *Call of the Minaret*, 263.

[151]Rahman, *Major Themes of the Qur'an*, 170.

The Nicene fathers thought that such a theological development engendered by the influence of Greek philosophy threatened the very essence of Christianity because it asserted that the Reality revealed and encountered in Jesus was different from God and therefore not the same as God. One would always question whether one day God might act and be revealed in a totally different manner from what one encountered in Jesus Christ. God might not be the one who willed to be vulnerable even unto death for the sake of humanity. The Nicene confessionalists therefore insisted that Jesus is God, Light of Light, very God of very God. One could trust that God is trustworthy. There is, nor would be, no other God than the Ultimate Reality incarnate in Jesus.[152]

When Christian-Muslim discussions focus on the preexistence of the Word which became flesh in Jesus Christ (Jn 1:1-14) or upon the divine nature of Christ, it should be noted that similar discussions have taken place within the Muslim community concerning the Qur'an. The Mutazilites (ninth century) argued that the Qur'an was created by God. They debated with those who argued that the Qur'an was eternal sharing the perfection of God's speech. The Mutazilites were concerned that a form of Qur'anic incarnationalism would slip into Islam. Eventually the understanding of the Qur'an as eternal was accepted within the Muslim community. Christians may appeal to this tradition as a way of making some analogies concerning the pre-existence and divinity of the Cosmic Crucified.[153]

The Christian community wishes to say that statements concerning the incarnation are statements of the unity of God. There is one God who is Revealer (Father), Revelation (Son incarnate) and Revealedness (the Spirit of Father and Son who enlightens and empowers the body of Christ in God's mission in the world).[154]

This affirmation of the unity of God may not be that which Muslims deny. Some Christians may agree when the Qur'an states that Jesus will be asked on the Day of Judgment whether he had taught trinitarianism to his followers, and he shall reply, "Glory be to Thee! Never could I say

---

[152]For some Muslims this would not be a significant point. Dr. Willem Bijlefeld quotes Dr. Isma'il Al-Faruqi who once said, "God does not reveal himself. He does not reveal himself to anyone in anyway. God reveals only His will." (From "God and Jesus: Theological Reflections for Christian-Muslim Dialog," 73.)

[153]Frederick Mathewson Denny, *An Introduction to Islam* (New York: Macmillian Publishing, 1985), 201-202.

[154]This particular Trinitarian terminology is derived from Karl Barth, *Church Dogmatics: The Doctrine of the Word of God*, vol. 1 (Edinburgh: T. & T. Clark, 1936), 417.

what I had no right (to say). Had I said such a thing, Thou wouldst Indeed have known it" (Surah 5:116). A trinitarian affirmation of God's unity is not rooted in Jesus' own words but in the church's convictions concerning the cosmic finality of Jesus Christ, which is expressed in Jesus' own words (Mt 11:25-27, Lk 10:21-24, Lk 11:29-32), and how that finality needed to be expressed in a hellenistic culture that questioned the capacity of the "Highest God" to be passionately wrapped up in human existence.

Fazlur Rahman quotes the Qur'anic invitation to community within the unity of God: "O People of the Book! Let us come together upon a formula which is common between us–that we shall not serve anyone but God, that we shall associate none with Him" (Surah 3:64)."[155]

Christians affirm the same unity within the reality of God; however, they see the one God through the window of Jesus the Cosmic Crucified. Through that window faith sees into the heart of the universe, from whence the creator of cosmic unity reintegrates and restores the world through the power of self-giving vulnerability incarnate in the Cosmic Crucified. Christians who acknowledge that ultimate truth will be called by the Triune God into self-giving, vulnerable life conformed to Christ for the sake of God's reconciling mission in the world.

C. The Vindication of the Prophet

According to most Muslims, the Qur'an states that Jesus did not die on the cross. In Surah 4 a number of charges are brought against the Jewish community, "The people of the Book" who have Moses as prophet (Surah 4:153ff). One of those accusations reads:

> That they said (in boast)
> "We killed Christ Jesus
> The Son of Mary,
> The Messenger of Allah"–
> But they killed him not,
> Nor crucified him,
> But so it was made
> To appear to them, . . .

---

[155]Rahman, *Major Themes of the Qur'an*, 170.

> For of a surety
> They killed him not—
> Nay, Allah raised him up
> Unto Himself; and Allah
> Is Exalted in Power, Wise-"
> (Surah 4:157-158)

Christians must recognize that Muslims deny the crucifixion of Jesus because they recognize Jesus as a messenger of God, and messengers of God are vindicated by God in this life as well as in the Day of Judgment. Dr. Fazlur Rahman writes, "Divine succor and final victory belongs to God's Messengers and those who support them: 'We do, indeed, help our Messengers and the believers in this life as well as on the Day when the Witnesses shall stand up'" (Surah 40:51).[156]   Rahman argues that this Qur'anic theme of victory of good over evil leads to the vindication of the Messengers of Allah. This theological conviction is the basis for "the rejection by the Qur'an of the crucifixion story."[157]

From a Muslim perspective, the New Testament account of the crucifixion is corrected to indicate that some unknown person resembling Jesus was put to death in his stead. From a Christian perspective, Kenneth Cragg writes that Islam has robbed Jesus of his own identity as the Cosmic Crucified. "The Jesus of the Gospels is undiscernible in the shadowy figure who is made to quit the path of his own teaching ['the Son of Man must suffer'] and his own *islam*, or 'surrender,' to the redeeming purpose of God. Truly here at the Muslim Cross we must say, as was said of old: 'They know not what they do.'"[158]

The understanding of Jesus' crucifixion is the crucial parting of the ways between Christians and Muslims. For Muslims the suffering and death of Allah's Messenger is not appropriate to God's presence and action, God's power and glory. God "cannot be thought not to rescue his servant from the hands of his enemies."[159]   From the Muslim perspective, vulnerability unto death is not appropriate for the kingdom/reign of God.

---

[156]Rahman, *Major Themes of the Qur'an*, 86.

[157]Rahman, *Major Themes of the Qur'an*, 87.

[158]Cragg, *The Call of the Minaret*, 268.

[159]Cragg, *The Call of the Minaret*, 268.

The Christian faith asserts precisely the opposite; namely, that God has chosen in the Cosmic Crucified to be vulnerable even unto death. This divine vulnerability even unto death is the very ground of our salvation.

This discussion clarifies for both Muslims and Christians how we believe in one God differently. "We are left with simple witness and the conviction we cannot enforce but only explain that 'God was in Christ reconciling the world unto himself.'"[160]

D. Islam and Social-Political Structures

The origins of Islam, unlike Christianity, are traced to revelation given to a person who was recognized not only as a prophet but also as a political leader.[161] Muhammad's prophetic ministry began in the city of Mecca; however, due to opposition to his work, Muhammad and his followers moved to Medina (622 A.D.). In Medina, Muhammad became the leader of a social-political community, and the revelatory messages received by Muhammad were filled with divine directives concerning community life.

Fazlur Rahman writes: "There is no doubt that the Qur'an wanted Muslims to establish a political order on earth for the sake of creating an egalitarian and just moral-social order."[162] Muslims inevitably integrate religion and social-political order because the Qur'an, as Allah's revelation, integrates all of life, individual and corporate, under the will of Allah.

Nations as well as individuals are called to submission to the will of God. H. A. R. Gibb writes that this original integration of religion and social-political life in Muhammad's life remained a basic motif within the Muslim community down through its history. "The connection between law and religion thus established by Mohammed and adopted by his followers persisted throughout all later centuries."[163]

Revelation is the grounds for the social-political order. The Qur'anic revelation supplemented by the *Hadith* (the traditions focused upon Muhammad) and later Muslim legal interpretations of the revelatory

---

[160]Cragg, *The Call of the Minaret*, 268.

[161]W. Montgomery Watt entitles his book on Muhammad, *Muhammad: Prophet and Statesman* (Oxford: Oxford University Press, 1961).

[162]Rahman, *Major Themes of the Qur'an*, 62.

[163]H. A. R. Gibb, *Mohammedanism: An Historical Survey*, 2nd ed. (1949; Reprint, New York: Oxford University Press, 1962), 90.

base are to be the legal basis for Muslim people. This totality is designated *Sharia*, the law. How then does the community as a nation endeavor to live in conformity to the will of Allah and to seek that Allah's will be done on earth? This is essential because the Muslim community is "charged with 'being witnesses upon mankind' and 'calling to goodness and prohibiting evil'" (Surah 2:143; 3:104, 110).[164] Fazlur Rahman answers the previous question with the Islamic concept *jihad*, which "is a total endeavor, an all-out effort—'with your wealth and lives,' as the Qur'an frequently puts it—to 'make God's cause succeed'" (Surah 9:40).[165]

Muslims speak of a greater and lesser *jihad*. The greater struggle is the person's inner struggle to live in submission to the will of Allah; the outer struggle is the effort to make God's cause succeed within the corporate society. Muslim peoples and leaders are called to seek the will of God's law in society. Political leaders are to establish worship and pay the poor their due and enjoin kindness and forbid iniquity (Surah 22:41).

Fazlur Rahman addresses Muslims' critics with these fascinating words:

> But when human religio-social endeavor is envisaged in the terms in which we have understood the Qur'an, *jihad* becomes an absolute necessity. How can such an ideological world-order be brought into existence without such a means? Most unfortunately, Western Christian propaganda has confused the whole issue by popularizing the slogan 'Islam was spread by the sword' or 'Islam is a religion of the sword.' What was spread by the sword was not the religion of Islam, but the *political domain* of Islam, so that Islam could work to produce the order on the earth that the Qur'an seeks. One may concede that *jihad* was often misused by later Muslims whose primary aim was territorial expansion and not the ideology they were asked to establish; one must also admit that the means of *jihad* can vary—in fact, armed *jihad* is only one form. But one can never say that 'Islam was spread by the sword.' There is no single parallel in Islamic history to the forcible conversion to Christianity of the German tribes *en masse* carried out by

---

[164]Rahman, *Major Themes of the Qur'an*, 53.

[165]Rahman, *Major Themes of the Qur'an*, 64.

Charlemagne, with repeated punitive expeditions against apostates–although, of course, locally and occasionally isolated cases of such conversions may well have taken place.[166]

Islam works "to produce the order on earth that the Qur'an seeks." This concept raises crucial issues wherever Muslims live with non-Muslim minorities or with non-Muslim majorities. In the southern Sudan, Indonesia and Malaysia, minority Christians feel threatened by the imposition or potential imposition of *Sharia*. In Nigeria almost equally large populations of Muslims and Christians debate the role of *Sharia* within constitutional government, and Christians debate their own role within a constitutional state. In India and the U.S.A., minority Muslim populations seek to adapt to a world in which Muslim law cannot function as a political reality; however, some Muslims will see good constitutional law based upon justice as a manifestation of God's law within society.

Rahman wishes to make a distinction between the Muslim religion and the Muslim political domain. He advocates, as the Qur'an does, religious freedom. The Qur'an states, "There is no compulsion in religion" (Surah 2:256). On the other hand, he believes that the will of God calls for untiring efforts to work toward a society that lives in conformity to the will of God. Political power and all other efforts are to be used to realize a just social order. Rahman is critical of Christianity because he believes it never envisions any social order.[167]

There is no consensus within the Christian community in regard to the relationship between the gospel and social-political structures. There have been Christians who, like Muslims, have seen the Christian community as God's instrument for ordering society in Jesus' name. Thomas Müntzer would represent a radical example of that understanding. There have been other Christians whose discipleship to the Cosmic Crucified have led them to renounce any use of force to impose God's will on the community. The Lutheran tradition, with its understanding of God's two-kingdom operation, normally attempts to take Jesus' own nonviolent ministry as normative for certain dimensions of life but not all of life. This debate continues within the Christian community even while we become more fully engaged with the Muslim world, which also is being challenged to rethink its traditional understanding of *Sharia* within new contexts.

---

[166]Rahman, *Major Themes of the Qur'an*, 63-64.

[167]Rahman, *Major Themes of the Qur'an*, 63.

Christians and Muslims are being forced to think together on this extremely difficult but essential topic because our common human future depends upon it. In some parts of the world, as in Nigeria, we must share our common concerns for life or we will share mutual annihilation.

As Christians enter this dialogue, they will recognize that they are to be conformed to that one who in love was willing to be vulnerable even unto death. Discipleship to the Cosmic Crucified within the Muslim world is an awesome and humbling privilege and task.

6

THE UNIQUE THEOLOGICAL TASK OF ENGAGING WITH BUDDHIST PEOPLES IN DIALOGUE AND WITNESS

Participation in the mission of the crucified Jesus within a Theravada Buddhist community confronts the Christian witnessing community with a unique and fascinating challenge. It is unique in that Theravada Buddhism articulates a religious view of life without reference to the reality of God. It is fascinating in that its view of life and values are in some ways similar to those reflected in Jesus' life and preaching.

Theravada Buddhism sees cosmic life as a pulsating totality of interdependent experiences and events. Persons, for example, are a confluence of what are termed the five aggregates (collections of substances, sensations, perceptions, volitional activities, and awarenesses), which are in continual flux. The primary presupposition is that underlying this flow of experiences and events experienced as "self or selves" there is no substantive ego or eternal soul. In a similar way there is no ultimate soul/substance that underlies "the cosmic independent fluctuating totality." Furthermore, all metaphysical questions concerning the finitude or infinitude of the totality or even the existence or nonexistence of the Enlightened One after death are metaphysical speculations that have no value in seeking the enlightened path of the Buddha.

In the world of Theravada, philosophical Buddhism, or Zen Buddhism, the Christian encounters persons for whom God is not real or relevant for salvation. That presents an intriguing challenge because the Christian community is forced to reexamine its primary presupposition and defend the reality of God, which is the foundation of the faith.

This challenge is so attractive and disturbing because the values of compassion, love, integrity, and nonviolence espoused by the Buddha are similar to the values embodied and articulated by Jesus of Nazareth. Furthermore, these values are espoused within a philosophy of life that views the world similarly to the Christian perspective.

126

The Buddha saw life primarily as suffering (*dukkha*). The world is marked by pain, loss, and impermanence. There are times of love, joy, peace, and happiness; however, they are never permanent and therefore are followed by loss and grief. Suffering or *dukkha* is essential to life, and enlightened analysis sees that suffering is caused by "selfish" desiring, craving, thirsting. On one level this is reflected in the human desire to live at the expense of the suffering of other persons. On a deeper level suffering is caused by all desire, whether it be selfish, altruistic, or idealistic, for all desire is that dimension of human experience which, because it seeks consequences, continues to imprison life within suffering. However, desire can be eliminated; therefore liberation from suffering is possible. One can eliminate *dukkha* in the realization of *nirvana*, the still point where thirsting and suffering cease.

This analysis reflects motifs similar to the Christian understanding of sin and sin's consequences. Sin is often defined as centering one's life in self or the collective self, rather than in God revealed in Jesus. Lives centered in self or anything less than the God of love result in sin-filled consequences, which result in life filled with pain and suffering. Even though Christians and Buddhists find release from suffering in different ways, they both recognize that suffering is integrally related to a person's primary relationship with God or ultimate reality. Both are also powerful advocates of compassion within the suffering of life. From the Christian perspective, the crucified Jesus places God in the middle of suffering and sees God in Jesus participating in a passionate and compassionate struggle to bring life into the midst of death.

A. Truth as Walk/Path or Truth as Gift (Grace)

A Buddhist scholar who had devoted several years of study to Christian theology was asked: "What have you found that most clearly distinguishes Buddhist and Christian approaches to truth?" He replied, "In Buddhism everything depends upon myself or us, while in Christianity everything depends upon God or upon grace." The Buddha is reported to have said, "One is one's own refuge, who else could be the refuge?"[168] The Buddha is understood to be the first person of our age to have discovered the way to liberation/release from suffering, but each one must walk the path alone.

---

[168]Walpola Sri Rahula, *What the Buddha Taught* (New York: Grove Press, 1974), 1.

This focus upon human responsibility for walking the way of liberation is fundamental within Theravada Buddhism. It is also a necessity because the human community is not accompanied by God as the Cosmic Companion. For Theravada Buddhism, God is either nonexistent or irrelevant in matters of salvation.

Within this Buddhist context, the message of God's grace—namely, that God in Christ shares the suffering of the human community, becomes vulnerable to death for the human community, and conquers death to transform the broken community and the cosmos—is heard as the consequence of psychological projections or hallucinations. These Christian beliefs are "strange" but understandable attempts to find peace and security in the fantasies of the human mind rather than facing the reality that we are responsible for walking our own path to liberation or *nirvana*.

There is this remarkable distinction between truth as *walk* and *truth* as *gift*.

It should be observed that later developments within Mahayana Buddhism spoke of *bodhisattvas* who forfeited for themselves entrance to *nirvana* in order to bring deliverance to suffering people. This particular movement toward grace reached its climax in Japan in a "Pure Land" form of Buddhism taught by Shinran (1173-1262).

Paul Martinson describes this development:

> For Shinran human depravity and lostness in ignorance, craving, and self was so deep and sustained that no self-effort leading to salvation was possible. The only hope was for an act of grace that came from the outside. This act was the ancient vow (promise) of the Amida Buddha eons ago that he not attain enlightenment unless all other beings also be guaranteed enlightenment thereby. That guarantee was to be theirs with only the simple calling on his name.[169]

Zen Buddhism, another form of Mahayana Buddhism developed in Japan, reflects the original Buddhist vision of finding refuge in oneself. A popular quote from Zen illustrates this fact. "If you meet the Buddha on the road, kill him." Here once again one confronts the distinction between

---

[169]Paul Martinson, "Do Our Pathways Cross?" *Suffering and Redemption: Exploring Christian Witness Within a Buddhist Context* (Collection of papers prepared by The American Lutheran Church's Board for World Mission and Inter-Church Cooperation Task Force on Christian Witness Among Buddhists, Minneapolis, Minnesota, 1986-88, Photocopied), 93 (hereafter cited as *Suffering and Redemption*).

truth as walk/path and truth as gift. Daisetz Teitaro Suzuki, the Japanese Zen scholar, writes: "For whatever authority there is in Zen, all comes from within."[170]

B. The Reality of the Totality or God - Creation

A Buddhist-Christian seminar on religion and suffering was held in Chicago in December 1991. One of the sessions dealt with Christian and Buddhist involvement in development work. A Christian, in addressing this topic, used the term "creation." A Buddhist scholar immediately raised his hand to speak and then stated that the term "creation" implied a Christian faith statement concerning the Creator. Because the Buddhists at the table did not see reality in those dualistic terms, he requested that a neutral term such as "nature" or "natural environment" be used in the discussion of development. In a later discussion, centered upon Christian chaplaincy work within hospitals, a Lutheran pastor spoke of sharing the love of God with the sick and dying. Once again a Buddhist participant's hand went up. He stated that his Buddhist students often asked, "Why do Christians find it necessary to state that God loves them when they are surrounded by the love of people?" These Theravada Buddhist questions indicate a second difference between the Buddhist and Christian visions of reality. For Christians, God is encountered as the Other, the awesome Wholly Other, who in costly love is passionately involved in human existence. For Buddhism, God as the encountered Wholly Other is nonexistent or irrelevant to salvation.

Walpola Sri Rahula, the Theravada Buddhist scholar, writes:

According to Buddhism, our ideas of God and Soul are false and empty. Though highly developed as theories, they are all the same extremely subtle mental projections, garbed in an intricate metaphysical and philosophical phraseology.[171]

The denial of God and soul is grounded in the Buddhist vision of reality as the sum total of all events and relationships behind which there are no eternal entities or identities. Behind the sum of the five aggregates

---

[170]Daisetz Teitaro Suzuki, *An Introduction to Zen Buddhism* (New York: Grove Press, 1964), 44.

[171]Rahula, *What the Buddha Taught*, 52.

(matter, sensations, perceptions, mental formations, consciousness) which are experienced as "myself" there is no permanent, eternal "Soul" or "Ego."[172] My experienced self is simply the fusion of those five aggregates at this particular present time. In the same way there is no permanent Cosmic-Self (God-Atman) behind the flux of the sum total of all reality.

Christians and other theists have often argued that everything must have a cause, and there must then be a First Cause, God. But when Christians are asked, "Where then does God come from?" the answer is simply, God is the Uncaused Mysterious Cause behind life who needs no cause. The Buddhist replies, if logically God can be an uncaused mystery, why cannot the "sum total of all reality" be an uncaused mystery. Like the presumed God, it is simply "there." Whether this Uncaused Reality is eternal or not eternal, finite or infinite, are speculative questions of no relevance for the path of liberation/deliverance which results in *nirvana.*[173]

Christian-Muslim discussions center in the nature of God. Discussions with Theravada Buddhists center in the reality of God. Why as Christians do we speak of God? What can we say to the Theravada Buddhist concerning the grounds of our vision, our conviction that we as the human community are accompanied by the awesome Cosmic Companion, God!

Traditionally, Christian theists have argued for the existence of God by arguing from cause to the First Cause; from contingency to Ultimate Necessity; from design to the Designer; from the claim of values or the sense of "ought" to the One who makes those claims or commands the ought; from the giftedness of existence to the Giver of existence.[174]

The Buddhist may respond that causal relationships simply "are" and need no First Cause any more than God necessitates the creator of God. Contingency simply is and needs no Ultimate Necessity, or contingency is the Ultimate necessity. Design is simply a mark of the cosmic totality, which is a given mystery of design much the same way that God is concluded by the theists to be the given Designer Mystery. And values are simply recognized as good and need no ground in the Value Giver. When the Christian argues that life is experienced as a given, implying a Giver, the Buddhist may reply that life as the sum total of reality is itself the

---

[172]Rahula, *What the Buddha Taught,* 20ff.

[173]Rahula, *What the Buddha Taught,* 13.

[174]Paul Sponheim, "To Know God in Experience," *Suffering and Redemption,* 106ff.

giftedness requiring no Giver. However, the Buddhist may reply that life is not giftedness at all because life is ultimately marked by suffering, which is the given from which one seeks release.

In this manner, the Buddhist may reject the traditional arguments for God as logically not necessary. However, in response the Christian theist may see in them testimony to the reality of God. They may appear as evidence much in the same way as circumstantial evidence is brought into a courtroom. They are not logically conclusive proof, but they may be seen by the Christian theist as signs of the reality of God. The givenness and giftedness of life are testimony pointing to the Giver of life. The design and meaningfulness of existence are testimony pointing to the Designer of life. The contingency of life points to that lying behind contingency, the Ultimate Necessity. In summary, in the experiences of giftedness, meaning and contingency, faith sees the Giver, the Designer, the Ultimate Necessity, God. It should be noted that there are a few persons continuing to call themselves Christians who have rejected theism and view reality in the unitary sense found in the Buddhist vision. For them God designates the dimension of reality that is experienced as the awesome givenness, meaning and mystery of it all.

Having shared this metaphysical debate, the Christian must state that the biblical faith did not arise out of a theological conversation or dialogue. Rather, the biblical and apostolic faith arose out of a faith encounter with God. In the voice of the prophets, the people of Israel with "ears to hear" heard and encountered the speaking God. In the events of Israel's history, such as the Exodus and the destruction of Jerusalem, those who had "eyes to see" saw the action of God. In the life, death and resurrection of Jesus, the "eyes of faith" saw and encountered the presence, the voice and activity of God. In Israel's and the church's worshipful (Psalms), reasonable (Wisdom, Epistles), missionary (Prophets, Epistles) response to God, the "eyes and ears" of faith encountered God. God was that awesome, gracious, disturbing Reality that called, empowered, comforted, challenged, and led a people who had "eyes to see and ears to hear." God called through an inner voice or in the words of a fellow human (prophet). God in and through events saved (Exodus), judged (fall of Jerusalem) and challenged (rebuild Jerusalem's walls). In the Cosmic Crucified, God called, forgave, challenged, empowered, comforted, saved. In and through the experiences of life, the "eyes and ears" of faith encountered the living God.

It was this experience of the encountered One, that One who stood over against the human community, that was ultimately the grounds for speaking of God. Abraham, Moses, Isaiah, Jeremiah, Jesus, Peter, Paul, and all persons of faith have encountered that gracious and disturbing Reality who unsettled their lives, made them restless with their own souls and their communities, and who ultimately gave them meaning and security within the brokenness and suffering of human existence. People of faith point to this divine-human encounter as the ground of talk of God.[175]

The most powerful testimony of God's over-againstness of reality is faith's encounter with Jesus' resurrection from the dead. Death is the universal mark of human and biological existence. Death seems inevitably to follow life. The resurrection runs counter to that universal order and as such is testimony to God as that reality who is encountered in the midst of life in Jesus Christ.[176]

The Buddhist may readily account for these experiences as psychological constructs interpreting natural human experiences or simply hallucinations of human communities who find it impossible to face the reality of human suffering or to take responsibility for one's own deliverance.

As Christians who have the privilege of seeing and hearing God in and through the flow of human existence, we live in amazing gratitude for the eyes that see and the ears that hear. The questions of possible hallucination are not met by counter charges of blindness and rebellion. Rather, they are met by the challenge to witness to the presence and action of God within the human family, the life of Israel, and the incarnate Cosmic Crucified in order that others, in faith, may encounter that God who is passionately involved in their lives and who went through hell for their own sake.

C. *Dukkha* (Suffering) or Sin and Its Consequences

Christianity and Buddhism perceive existence in similar terms. Both understand existence other than one would desire or hope it to be. The Buddha's teaching centers in the Four Noble Truths:

1. *Dukkha*
2. The arising/origin of *dukkha*

---

[175]See Appendix 1.

[176]See Wolfhart Pannenberg; *Jesus--God and Man*, trans. by Lewis L. Wilkens and Duane A. Priebe (Philadelphia: Westminister Press, 1968), chapter 3, particularly page 131. For a critical affirmation of Pannenberg's thesis see Mark Thomsen, "The Lordship of Jesus and Theological Pluralism," *Dialog*, vol. 9, 1972, 125ff.

3.   The cessation of *dukkha*
4.   The way leading to the cessation of *dukkha*[177]

The Four Noble Truths revolve around *dukkha*, a Pali word meaning suffering, pain, sorrow, misery, in contrast to happiness. Buddhist scholars note that the word has deeper connotations within a religious discussion, such as imperfection, impermanence, and emptiness. According to Walpola Rahula, the word "realistically" designates life as it is and is the point from which one longs for that which is hoped and desired: freedom, peace, tranquility.

This does not mean that the Buddhist does not recognize experiences of happiness such as family happiness, friendship happiness, aesthetic pleasure; however, these experiences of happiness are not permanent. They come and go, and with their passing comes a sense of sadness and loss. Furthermore, life is marked by many types of pain, both mental and physical, such as oppression, poverty, enslavement, loneliness and conflict caused by greed, hate, tyranny, etc. Buddhism basically sees life characterized by *dukkha* as that from which the thoughtful person will seek liberation or deliverance.

In a somewhat similar manner, Christianity views life as marked by suffering and brokenness. Life is marked by estrangement, alienation, loneliness, strife, conflict, lovelessness, meaninglessness. From the Christian perspective, life is not as God intends it to be, as it was, as it ought to be, nor as it will be! Christian thought understands this suffering and brokenness to be rooted in sin and its consequences.

Sin is described as a state of being in which God and God's will are not accepted as the center/basis for life. Humanity, rather than centering in God, trusting God, obeying God, determines to center in (trust in or obey) something less than God, whether it be nation, family or the individual self. This primal stance with or against the God who is compassionately and creatively involved in life has consequences for every dimension of life.[178]

For example, trust and obedience in God (centering in God) who has created and loves the whole human family and who intends the human family to live in love and trust of each other means that humanity will be

---

[177]Rahula, *What the Buddha Taught,* 16ff, for a description of *dukkha*.

[178]George Forell, *The Protestant Faith* (Englewood Cliffs: Prentis-Hall, 1960), 133ff; Paul Tillich, "Existence and the Christ," *Systematic Theology* (Chicago: University of Chicago Press, 1957), vol. 2, 44ff.

called and empowered to love and trust each other. Centering in God will mean centering in God's human family. Turning from God in distrust (unfaith) and disobedience will mean a breach in the God-human relationship, but it will also result in broken relationships between persons. This interdependency of relationships is seen in the creation-fall accounts in Genesis 1-2. When Adam and Eve break their relationship with God, they are estranged from each other. They make themselves clothing, signifying their estrangement, and Adam blames his fallen state upon Eve, who had been given to him as God's intended companion (a state of alienation).

One can similarly note that in moving from being God-centered (faith) to other than God centered, humanity moves from innocence to guilt, from living relationships to alienation; from trusting responsibility to God and God's children to irresponsibility; from *shalom* to destructive conflict, from creative servanthood to exploitive domination; and from life to death. Life is broken; suffering and pain are essential marks of human existence. In biblical terms, people long for their liberation, their deliverance, their redemption.

This realistic perspective on the tragedy of human existence is shared by Buddhists and Christians. We have very a different vision of humanity's ultimate liberation; however, we do share common convictions concerning the necessity of our compassionate involvement with people on behalf of a common struggle for justice and peace within the tragedies of life.

D. Buddhist Denial of the Ego or Christian Self-Denial

Christian discipleship is Jesus' call to "deny themselves and take up their cross and follow me. For those who want to save their life will lose it, and those who lose their life for my sake, and for the sake of the gospel, will save it" (Mk 8:34-35). Jesus calls his disciples to deny themselves—to say no to themselves—in order that they may say yes to God in the Cosmic Crucified. In our earlier discussion dealing with being conformed to Jesus Christ, we noted that in Paul and Luther there is the declaration that the "old" self which does not wish to be conformed to God's will must die in order that the "new" self wishing to be conformed to God's will might rise or come to life.

Christian self-denial is a surrender to God and God's will. It is surrender to the God-in-Christ-centered life in order to become a Cosmic Crucified-centered life. Christian self-denial has at times deteriorated into an attitude in which one despises oneself. Within early Christianity, influenced by Gnosticism which elevated spirit and despised matter, people became disgusted with their existence as flesh and blood. The flesh was to be despised and neglected as one, for example, lived in filth or one remained celibate, being uninvolved in the fleshly things of life. Within medieval Christianity with its focus upon guilt and the terror of judgment, one, in self-denial, tormented the sinful self through disciplines of fasting or self-flagellation in order to purify the soul. These examples of self-denial are distortions of Jesus' call to discipleship, to conformity with Christ.

Christian self-denial is the call of the Cosmic Crucified to say no to self, to anything less than God, in order to say yes with one's whole being to God. Protestant theology has emphasized that human pride is often that which stands in the way of self-surrender to God. Human pride must die that Christ might be Lord of life.[179]   Contemporary forms of liberation theology have noted that persons may not only see themselves as "more than" God intends them to be (pride) but they may see themselves as "less than" God intends them to be (self-effacement). Persons may deny their God-given value and giftedness. In this case, self-denial means saying no to one's denial of one's own value and giftedness in order that one can say yes to God's call to serve Jesus Christ with one's God-given gifts.

The Buddhist also speaks of denying the self, but in totally different terms. When Buddhism speaks of the non-substantiality of the ego or the doctrine of the No-Soul (*Anatta*), it does not speak in terms of a spiritual and moral encounter with God, but rather speaks of a metaphysical fact.[180] Buddhism begins with an analysis of the self and comes to the conclusion that the self is a confluence of the five aggregates underlying which there is no lasting entity that can be designated the self or the soul.

Christian self-denial is a surrender of one's life to the mission of God that sweeps one into the world in order that one might participate in God's mission to transform the totality of reality. Buddhist denial of the self is a recognition of the metaphysical insight that the self is ultimately a transient reality, which makes release from the cycle of suffering (*samsara*) possible.

---

[179]Reinhold Niebuhr, *The Nature and Destiny of Man: A Christian Interpretation*, vol. 1 (New York: Charles Scribner's Sons, 1955), chapter 7, 186ff.

[180]Rahula, *What the Buddha Taught*, 50ff.

E. *Nirvana* or **Resurrection and a New Creation**

For the Buddhist, *nirvana* is liberation, deliverance from *dukkha* and is the awakening enlightenment. The Four Noble Truths again are:

1. *Dukkha*
2. The arising/origin of *dukkha*
3. The cessation of *dukkha*
4. The way leading to the cessation of *dukkha* - *Nirvana*

Buddhism must be seen on the background of Hinduism, which envisions existence as a continual cycle of existence, including incarnations and reincarnations of the soul. This cycle of existence (*samsara*) is experienced as that from which one desires deliverance. Within this cyclical existence, the law of *karma* is at work, rewarding good and punishing evil. Living contrary to that which is good produces punishing consequences in future incarnations and vice versa. Ultimate deliverance within Hinduism occurs when the individual soul (*atman*) is recognized and experienced as one with the Cosmic Soul (*Atman*).

Buddhism assumes that existence is cyclical and *karma* is at work through experiences of reincarnation; however, as noted earlier, it rejects the reality of a permanent *atman* (soul) or *Atman* (God). Within this context, Buddhism begins with *dukkha* (the First Noble Truth).

This is followed by the Second Noble Truth which states that *dukkha* arises from thirst, craving, desire (*tanha*):

> It is this "thirst," which produces re-existence and re-becoming, and which is bound up with passionate greed, and which finds fresh delight now here and now there, namely, (1) thirst for sense pleasure, (2) thirst for existence and becoming and (3) thirst for non-existence.[181]

Thirst in the sense of greed often causes suffering for the exploited and also for the greedy. Thirst in the form of sensual desire causes the suffering of exploitation and abuse within sexual relationships. It must be noted, however, that Buddhism understands thirst in a much deeper and more comprehensive manner. Any desire to exist, to continue within the realm of *dukkha*, participates in and prolongs the unsatisfactoriness of

---

[181]Rahula, *What the Buddha Taught*, 29.

existence. A thirst for that which is beautiful or good also extends this existence. Paradoxically, even the thirst for nonexistence prevents one's awakening, the realization of *nirvana. Nirvana* is when thirst of any kind ceases.[182]

Nirvana may be realized in this life, or it may be realized in some future reincarnation, or in some "heavenly" dimension of existence. The famous Thai Buddhist monk Buddhadasa interestingly argues that enlightenment or the attainment of *nirvana* is more readily attained within the human state.

> The expression "happy state [*nirvana*]) in the human realm" signifies that in the human realm impermanence, unsatisfactoriness, and non-selfhood can more readily be perceived than in the celestial realm. In the human realm there are enlightened beings, there are *arahants* [enlightened ones], and there are the Buddha, Dhamma [teaching], and Sangha [the community]. In the celestial realm, that jungle of sensuality, there are none of these things. Thus, celestial beings come to the human realm in search of the happy state . . . Some people seek paradise, happiness in the next existence, in the realm of celestial beings. They invest in it by making merit, giving to charity, selling their houses and goods, and building things in monasteries. Where is the genuinely happy state to be found? Think it over.[183]

Buddhadasa makes it clear that *nirvana* is attainable here and now. *Nirvana* "is to be found in dying before death."[184] One should note that Buddhadasa is not always popular among many traditional Thai Buddhist monks.

When *nirvana* is realized, the forces which produced *dukkha*, the cyclical realm of suffering, cease because there is no more thirst for continuing existence. There is now a "still-point"; the cycle of suffering is followed by a indescribable and incomprehensible awakening that must be experienced to be known—*nirvana*.

---

[182]Rahula, *What the Buddha Taught*, 35.

[183]Buddhadasa Bhikkhu, *Buddha-Dhamma for Students, rev. ed.* (Bangkok: Dhamma Study and Practice Group, revised 1988), 52-53.

[184]Buddhadasa, *Buddha-Dhamma for Students*, 39.

Walpola Rahula in pointing to *nirvana* quotes several Pali texts:

He who has realized the Truth, *Nirvana*, is the happiest being in the
world. He is free from all "complexes" and obsessions, the worries
and troubles that torment others. His mental health is perfect. He
does not repent the past, nor does he brood over the future. He
lives fully in the present. Therefore he appreciates and enjoys things
in the purest sense without self-projections. He is joyful, exultant,
enjoying the pure life, his faculties pleased, free from anxiety, serene
and peaceful. As he is free from selfish desire, hatred, ignorance,
conceit, pride, and all such "defilements," he is pure and gentle, full
of universal love, compassion, kindness, sympathy, understanding and
tolerance. His service to others is of the purest, for he has no
thought of self. He gains nothing, accumulates nothing, not even
anything spiritual, because he is free from the illusion of Self, and
the "thirst" for becoming.[185]

Christianity views deliverance (salvation) very differently. In contrast
to the unitary view of existence envisioned by Buddhism, Christians believe
that they have encountered God. God in the Cosmic Crucified is the
Cosmic Companion who accompanies the human community through the
suffering of existence; the Cosmic Lord who disturbs and unsettles life
calling humanity to repentance and cruciform discipleship as God transforms
the totality of creation; the Cosmic Savior who was vulnerable to death in
order that humanity might be forgiven and reconciled to the Father/Mother
of life; the Cosmic Liberator who conquers death and leads God's people
into resurrection life.

In encountering God within creation and history, Christians trust
that all of life is rooted in God's creative and gracious action. God's
passionate concern for life, for people, righteousness and justice indicate
that all of life is from God; it is God's good creation. God's incarnation
in the flesh and blood of Jesus is indicative that all of life (physical,
psychological, spiritual) is of God and ultimately a created gift of God.
The resurrection of Jesus Christ, rather than spiritual or psychic
appearances of Jesus, is testimony that God ultimately is committed to the
transformation of a concrete world where "all God's children got shoes,"
and live in the illuminating presence of the God who dwells with God's
people.

---

[185]Rahula, *What the Buddha Taught*, 43.

Participation in this God-created cosmic reality, the resurrection life, is by invitation of Jesus the Cosmic Crucified. Like the grace of forgiveness, it is sheer gift. It is rooted in the resurrection of Jesus Christ[186] and is promised to those who are incorporated into his life and mission.

> Death has been swallowed up in victory.
> Where, O death, is your victory?
> Where, O death, is your sting?"

> The sting of death is sin, and the power of sin is the law. But thanks be to God, who gives us the victory through our Lord Jesus Christ.

> Therefore, my beloved, be steadfast, immovable, always excelling in the work of the Lord, because you know that in the Lord your labor is not in vain. (1 Cor 15:54-58)

A question is always raised within the context of this resurrection promise. Are only Christians given this promise? I still remember African students asking about the eternal destiny of parents or grandparents who had died before the preaching of the gospel.

The Christian celebration of the resurrection faith is not to be mistaken for the assertion that the eternal destiny of every person depends upon meeting this Jesus through the preaching of the gospel within history or being recognized members of our Christian institutions.

The Bible clearly states that to meet Jesus Christ is to have confronted judgment and life:

> Indeed, God did not send the Son into the world to condemn the world, but in order that the world might be saved through him. [those] who believe in him are not condemned; but [those] who [do] not believe are condemned already, ... this is the judgment, that the light has come into the world, and people loved darkness rather than light because their deeds are evil. (Jn 3:17-21)

This and similar passages make it clear that a positive or negative response to Jesus has present and eternal consequences. The Johannine passage, similar to many other biblical texts, makes assertions about those

---

[186] 1 Cor 15:20 where Jesus is "the first fruits of those who have died."

who have had the privilege of meeting Jesus. Those who have met Jesus and trusted in Jesus have already passed from darkness into light, from death to life. They already dwell within the incredible reality of God's truth incarnate in Jesus, the magnificence of the messianic reign of God in Christ. In the words of Romans 10:13-17, they have called upon the name of the Lord and have been saved.

John 3:17-21 and similar texts also indicate that those who have met Jesus and rejected God's truth incarnate in Jesus have already been judged as outside the messianic kingdom because they loved the darkness rather than the light. This text and similar texts do not make any statement about those who have not met the truth or seen the light in Jesus. They have not yet been through judgment. One can also state that there are many who have never met the truth and light of Jesus even though they have heard of Jesus. It seems probable that we as Christians have so distorted Jesus Christ that we have made it impossible for grace and truth (Jn 1:14) in Jesus to be known and experienced by those that we have oppressed and crushed or by those who cannot see Jesus in the entanglements of our theological or confessional statements. The contemporary Jewish community would certainly be one example.

Questions are always raised as to how God will ultimately deal with those who have never heard or who have misheard the gospel. One can leave that in the hands of God, knowing that the same compassion, grace, and forgiveness is offered to them as to us. Their salvation, like ours, will be grounded in the pain and suffering of God embodied in Jesus. When and where they will encounter the grace and judgment of Jesus can be left with God.

Many biblical passages indicate that the culminating feast and banquet will be much more inclusive than some Christians might expect. Jesus, having heard the words of a Roman centurion, said, "Truly I tell you, in no one in Israel have I found such faith. I tell you, many will come from east and west and will eat with Abraham and Isaac and Jacob in the kingdom of heaven, while the heirs of the kingdom will be thrown into the outer darkness" (Mt 8:10-11). In Luke 10, Jesus portrays life within the kingdom of God in the person of a heretical Samaritan. In Luke 18:9-14, an unknown sinner cries out for grace and unknowingly returns home justified before God. In John, Jesus states, "I have other sheep that do not belong to this fold. I must bring them also, and they will listen to my voice" (Jn 10:16).

Paul, speaking to Athenians, stated there are times of ignorance that God overlooks, not calling persons to accountability before Christ (Acts 17:30). In Romans 2 Paul writes that all humanity has the law of God written on their hearts which "will accuse or perhaps excuse them on the day when, according to my gospel, God, through Jesus Christ, will judge the secret thoughts of all" (Rom 2:15-16). Ephesians 1 speaks of a divine plan to gather all things in him, things in heaven and things on earth (Eph 1:9-10). The Apostle Peter writes of a mission of Christ to the realm of the imprisoned dead who had been disobedient in the times of Noah (1 Pt 3:18-20). In these passages there are enough inspired glimpses of the new heaven and new earth to indicate that God's future messianic banquet will have surprises for us all!

F. The Path Leading to the Cessation of *Dukkha* and the Way of the Cross

For the Christian, the way of the cross is primarily the Cosmic Crucified's way in the world; therefore, the way of the cross is God's way and God's walk through a broken and suffering world. Only secondarily is it our way in the world as God in Christ calls, renews and empowers us to be conformed to the Cosmic Crucified. In conformity to Christ, we are called and empowered to compassionate self-giving service, to vulnerability in mission, to a continuing struggle for peace, justice and wholeness of life.

The way or path within Theravada Buddhism is "my" path. As the young Buddhist said, "for Christians all depends upon God and God's grace, for Buddhists all depends upon us." Few Christians, however, would challenge the values called for by the Fourth Noble Truths, (The Path):

1. Right Understanding
2. Right Thought
3. Right Speech
4. Right Action
5. Right Livelihood
6. Right Effort
7. Right Mindfulness
8. Right Concentration

The path is devoted to ethical conduct, to mental discipline and wisdom. Walpola Rahula writes: "Ethical Conduct is built on the vast conception of universal love and compassion for all living beings, on which the Buddha's teaching is based."[187] He further states "that compassion

---

[187]Rahula, *What the Buddha Taught*, 46.

represents love, charity, kindness, tolerance and such noble qualities on the emotional side, or qualities of the heart." The Buddhist Path also includes qualities of the mind including mental discipline and wisdom.

The Buddhist understanding of the qualities of the heart, including love, compassion, charity and kindness, are strikingly similar to the values called for in Jesus' preaching and teaching. Christians immediately think of Jesus' parable of the Good Samaritan or Jesus' saying, "Love your neighbor as yourself" (Mt 19:19). Buddhists think of Buddha's sayings:

> One should win anger through kindness, wickedness through goodness, selfishness through charity and falsehood through truthfulness.[188]

However, that which is most nearly identical is the advocacy for non-violence by both Buddha and Jesus. Wapola Rahula writes:

> It is too well known to be repeated here that Buddhism advocates and preaches non-violence and peace as its universal message, and does not approve of any kind of violence or destruction of life. According to Buddhism there is nothing that can be called a "just war"—which is only a false term coined and put into circulation to justify and excuse hatred, cruelty, violence and massacre. Who decides what is just or unjust? The mighty and the victorious are "just," and the weak and the defeated are "unjust." Our war is always "just," and your war is always "unjust." Buddhism does not accept this position.[189]

The common emphasis upon compassion, love, kindness, nonviolence has on many occasions attracted Buddhists and Christians to each other. The Buddha has been an attractive figure for some Christians, and Jesus has been an attractive figure for some Buddhists.

The Buddhist Path includes qualities of the mind as well as qualities of the heart. They are both included within the same walk. One does not progress from one to the other; both are essential to the walk along which enlightenment may take place. In order to develop qualities of the mind, Buddhism emphasizes meditation, and meditation may be defined as mental development. There are two forms of meditation.

---

[188]Rahula, *What the Buddha Taught*, 86.

[189]Rahula, *What the Buddha Taught*, 84.

The first is the development of mental concentration. Various methods are used to focus the mind, leading to mystic states. Buddhism, however, does not regard the mystic states as "enlightenment." They are mind created or induced and have nothing to do with reality - *nirvana*. There, then, is a second form of meditation which is insight into the nature of things. This is insight into *dukkha*, the rise of *dukkha*, the cessation of *dukkha* leading to wisdom and "the complete liberation of the mind, to the realization of Ultimate Truth, *Nirvana*."[190]

Some Christians have been deeply impressed with the value of Buddhist meditation, the mental discipline and its healing effects upon the human personality. I would not question the value of this mental discipline. I believe that the Western activist mentality can learn from meditative disciplines of the East. Persons need time to stop and center one's being. However, ultimately Christian meditation will be different from Buddhist meditation in that one either perceives reality as Self-Walk or as an accompanied journey with the Cosmic Companion. Enlightenment comes when the walk ceases and the "still-point" is realized. God's walk, which passionately embraces creation and humanity, is realized in a new creation when all tears are wiped away and death, mourning, crying and pain will be no more for the first things have passed away (Rv 21:4).

These very different perspectives draw persons in different cosmic directions. The Buddhist perspective draws persons out of the cyclical, transient realm of *dukkha*. It draws them out of attachment to the cycle of suffering in order to realize that still-point where *dukkha* ceases. The Cosmic Crucified calls humanity into the pain and suffering in order that life and creation might be transformed as a new creation. As Buddhists and Christians are drawn in these different cosmic directions, they will often find that they share common visions and struggles for the alleviation of pain in the middle of life. Compassion is a mark of the Way of the Buddha as well as the Way of the Cross!

---

[190]Rahula, *What the Buddha Taught*, 68.

7
IMPLEMENTING MISSION AMONG MUSLIMS AND BUDDHISTS

"The primary task of Christ's church is to proclaim Jesus Christ as Savior and Lord." The previous chapters have indicated the cruciform content of this message and the cruciform lives of those who hear the message. The one proclaimed is Jesus the Cosmic Crucified, and through Jesus we believe that we know God. We believe that this knowing encounter with God through Christ enables us to trust that God is the faithful, self-giving One who is compassionately in our midst and who intentionally was vulnerable to death for our salvation.

To know God in this way is very different from knowing God through the Qur'an and its understanding of Allah. Living in response to God's costly grace is very different from living in response to Allah's merciful justice. Our confidence in the ultimate is different; our ethical response should also be different.

Knowing God in the Cosmic Crucified is also very different from experiencing enlightenment within Buddhism. Living in response to God's costly grace is very different from ultimately finding refuge in oneself. Following the Cosmic Crucified is a very different experience from following the Buddhist path, even though one often does the same things.

Living in response to God's costly grace is even more strikingly different from living in response to the image of God molded by powerful nations and peoples who in arrogance value military, financial and technological power. These are very different understandings of the Ultimate! We believe and will proclaim that Jesus Christ is Savior and Lord. We believe that we know God through Jesus crucified and risen. We will proclaim in order that others may believe.

Background

Our world of five billion people is deeply marred by sin and its consequences. Humanity has turned away from God and insists on walking its own disastrous way. Contrary to God's vision for human

144

life and creation, the world is permeated with enmity, greed, conflict, guilt and death and lies under the judgment of God. Broken and suffering, the world waits for its redemption.

The gospel announces that God in love sent Jesus Christ into the world as Savior to call for the world's repentance and to die for the sins of the world. Raised from death, Jesus Christ is God's victory over sin and death and is God's promise of a new creation.

There are two billion people who have not had the opportunity to hear this gospel. Another one and one-half billion persons have a minimal knowledge of Christ. There are, then, three and one-half billion persons who have not had the possibility of responding to God's saving gospel which promises justification by grace through faith in Jesus Christ and new life empowered by the Holy Spirit within the body of Christ; therefore:

Commitment

We are committed to proclaim to those who have not heard or who have not fully heard the gospel that Jesus Christ is Savior and Lord in order that they might believe. (Commitment 1 in Commitments for Mission in the 1990s)

A. Proclaiming That They May Believe

We believe that this knowing of God in the Cosmic Crucified is incredibly good news—Gospel! It is such good news that it might appear to be unbelievable in a world marked by brokenness, suffering and pain. In a world of suffering is it possible that God is Love (1 Jn 4:8)? Persons have always asked, "Can this possibly be true?" "Can the news be this good?" I have often said "I can understand why people in a world of suffering are agnostics or atheists; however, I cannot understand why people who believe in Jesus Christ do not want to speak about the gospel, share it, preach it in order that others might believe it."

I do, however, understand that the church has often so distorted Jesus the Cosmic Crucified that there are those who fear being identified with the distortion. People feel ashamed when the name of Jesus is used to fight wars, whether military, religious, political or ecclesiastical; exploit the marginalized, whether they are people of color, women, or those afflicted with AIDS; or ridicule the faith of Buddhists, Hindus, or Muslims.

Shame over these distortions should not lead to forfeiting the name of Jesus. The mission of the church must recapture the name of the Jesus of the New Testament. For it is through this Jesus the Cosmic Crucified that one sees and knows the heart of God There is no other revelation that knows God in this unique, unsurpassable way. Nowhere else does one encounter God who has shared the depths of brokenness and the hell of betrayal to death in order that we may have life. We preach Jesus Christ as Savior and Lord in order that persons may believe this gospel and walk in this light.

There will be some persons who denounce this missionary goal as a form of proselytism. One may be told that witnessing to Christ with the hope that persons might believe is illegitimate, because each faith community has its own legitimacy, and witness should seek only the enrichment of one another's faiths. We have observed that enrichment will always take place, because God is in the life of all people. However, we have also said that Buddhists, Muslims and Christians believe very differently. We are convinced that the gospel of Jesus Christ is a treasure beyond any price compared to the insights of other faiths. If it is actually a true treasure beyond any price as we believe, then the whole human community should have the privilege and even the right of believing it.

One cannot compel faith in Jesus Christ. It not only is psychologically impossible; it is absolutely contrary to the message and mission of Jesus crucified and risen. We are simply called to be witnesses to Jesus as God's final truth. God grants us the privilege of planting the seed of God's Word. We are then to allow the Spirit of God to bring forth the truth (Mk 4:1-20, Is 55:10-11).

We agree with critics of the missionary movement who reject proselytizing when defined as using external forces to compel Christian discipleship. Discipleship is not to be created by rewarding persons with social power, material benefits and gifts of any kind in order to facilitate conversions to Christianity. Much less should discipleship be sought by threat of misfortune, torture or death. The fact that the church has actually practiced such methods is both deplorable and at times horrifying. We have, however, shown that all such efforts are absolutely contrary to and condemned by Jesus the Cosmic Crucified.

A few years ago an Evangelical Lutheran Church in America missionary working in West Africa asked, "Frankly, I guess what I want to know is whether you want us to make disciples of Muslim peoples?" I wrote in response:

I have indicated that our work is rooted in the finality of Jesus as God's ultimate self-identification. There is no God other than the God who raised Jesus; therefore, there is no hidden or revealed God other than the vulnerable suffering God revealed in the abandoned and crucified one. For the Christian that is ultimate truth and ultimate grace; therefore, it must be shared. It must be shared not because the crucified one with imperial power threatens to crush or torment those who have not heard or believed, but because this incredible treasure of truth and grace must be offered to every person within the human community! Jesus insists that all are to share in the reality of God's kingdom embodied in Jesus: "Go . . . and make disciples of all nations, . . ." (Matt. 28:19). For the sake of every person who is destined to walk this planet, the treasure is not to be hidden! It must be proclaimed that God is ultimately compassion and grace. It must be shared that every broken and lonely individual so often lost within the wilderness of crowds and masses is passionately known and loved by God. It must be announced and known that whenever one broken soul in despair cries for forgiveness and hope in the night, that she or he, knowingly or not, is already forgiven and at peace with God, whose embrace has taken the form of arms with nail-pierced hands. In Jesus' name, it must be announced to those whose self-esteem has been crushed by religious and cultural oppression that they, too, have been created in the image of God and have gifts and potential yet undreamed of. It must be proclaimed to those who understand every tragedy and every tear as the consequence of God's hidden and capricious will, that God, although hidden, is absolutely and ultimately *for* them through the crucified and risen one. It must be announced to those who despair when compassion and justice are crushed and life is consumed by death that Jesus is raised as the first fruits of God's re-creation. Life will spring forth from death! This is the treasure that must be universally proclaimed.

God's call to repentance voiced and embodied in Jesus as prophet must also be universally announced. The prophetic voice of Jesus must be allowed to challenge every person, group, society, organization, and nation. Every person and every human structure in some way embodies the demonic principalities and powers that dehumanize the whole of creation and its peoples. Jesus as raised prophet spoke not only to ancient Galilean crowds but speaks to the teeming masses that inhabit the 250 nations claiming autonomy at the beginning of the 21st century. Wherever people and life are crushed, wherever love is absent, justice perverted, the good betrayed, and the beautiful disgraced, there the risen prophet must be enabled to speak. God's voice must be heard, "Repent, for the kingdom of God is at hand." People are to be challenged to repentance in Jesus' name. For the sake of their own life and for the sake of the lives they ignore and destroy, they are called to repentance. To those who in repentance know themselves as sinners, Jesus promises, "Your sins are forgiven; go in peace." To those who trust him Jesus is heard to say, "Take up your cross and follow me!"

My missionary friend may still ask, "But do you want us to make disciples out of Muslim people?" If you mean do you want the hearts and minds of our Muslim friends to be captured and molded by God who raised Jesus from the dead, then I desire that they be disciples! If you mean do you want Muslim people to find faith, hope, and love in God's incredible prophetic embodiment in Jesus, then I desire that they know and live within this truth! If you mean do you want them to be participants within a community of faith who, through the power of the God embodied in Jesus, live out their lives in mutual confession, affirmation, and mission, then I would hope that this could be a living reality for them. I also pray that they may find that reality within our Christian and Lutheran churches. However, if you mean do I insist that life and salvation can only be found in *membership* in our Christian or Lutheran churches, then I know that the traditional social structures of Islamic society, the historical tensions existing between our communities and the brokenness of our own Christian churches may make that an impossibility. It may mean that God intends to work out God's own future for Christians and Muslims in terms that we have not dreamed of. [It could be that Jesus might be received as Savior and Lord within the Muslim community in ways unknown and unexpected by us.]

Finally, as Christians who wish to share the cruciform message and mission of Jesus, and also as Christians who recognize the depths of our own brokenness and the brokenness of all humanity, we pray that we might at least fragmentarily be true and faithful in our witness to God's love and truth spoken and embodied in Jesus. Our claims to truth and faith are not claims of religious or spiritual superiority nor claims of future privileged positions in eternity. They are confessions of witnesses who believe that they have been captured by an ultimate and unsurpassable vision of universal truth, grace, and life, which God brings into existence through the crucifixion and resurrection of the prophet Jesus, the Cosmic Crucified. [They are confessions of those who pray and hope that others might believe.]

B. Organizing Churches and Congregations

As persons are grasped by the gospel and become believers, it is essential that they experience the privilege and necessity of community within the body of Christ. The Christian community is gathered (called out) from the human family by the call of Jesus Christ and they are gathered in Jesus name as the body of Christ (1 Corinthians 12). Within this community, Christ is present. "Where two or three are gathered in my name, I am there among them" (Mt 18:20). Christ is present, speaks, and acts as the Word of God incarnate in Jesus Christ is preached and taught. This preached and taught Word is made alive within the believers and community through the power of the Holy Spirit. The same Jesus Christ is present, speaks, and acts through the sacraments of Baptism and the Lord's Supper. Within our Lutheran community, these are the only essential unifying marks of the church: the teaching of that gospel and the administration of the sacraments. All else may be created to enable the local church to be freely and powerfully a new expression of the body of Christ. The Augsburg Confession, Article VII reads: "For the true unity of the church it is enough to agree concerning the teaching of the gospel and the administration of the sacraments. It is not necessary that human traditions or rites and ceremonies, instituted by men, should be alike everywhere." A more recent statement by Herbert Butterfield states this more powerfully: "Hold to Christ, and for the rest be totally uncommitted."[191]

Within this community (*koinonia*), there is to be: 1) a reconciled human family; 2) healing and nurture for the broken and suffering; and 3) the mandate and empowerment for mission. The visible church is both an actualization and distortion of this God-intended community, the body of Christ.[192]

Insofar as the church manifests the authentic body of Christ, it is a sign of God-given hope in the world.

---

[191]Herbert Butterfield, *Christianity and History* (New York: Charles Scribner's Sons, 1949), 146.

[192]Paul Tillich, *Systematic Theology*, vol. 3 (Chicago: University of Chicago Press, 1963), 155.

1. Centers of Reconciled Community Within Human Alienation

The world is marred by enmity and alienation. Individuals, families, communities and nations distrust, compete, struggle and destroy one another. Human lives and history seem to be a continual narrative of conflict with intervals of peace. The consequences of this global estrangement are incredible suffering and pain. Estranged persons live out their lives in loneliness. Alienated persons consign one another to pain, poverty and oppression. Enmity results in strife, war and the death of millions.

The world hungers for reconciliation and unity. It longs for peace the cessation of hostilities, quiet streets and silent nights. The world dreams of what Scripture describes as a new creation or new heavens and a new earth.

Within this search for unity, the church is called to be a sign of reconciliation and hope. The church is a reconciled community. God was in Christ reconciling the world unto himself and reconciling those at enmity with each other. In Christ there is neither male nor female, slave nor free, Jew nor Gentile. God in Christ has broken down all the walls of separation. In conformity to Jesus the Cosmic Crucified, we are called to cross all boundaries in order to share God's embrace of the world.

As a church we are called to participate more fully in the unity of the body of Christ as a sign of hope. We are called to be a community in which all the walls of separation are challenged and ultimately destroyed. Racism, sexism, nationalism, denominationalism are all to be challenged in order that the church might be a sign of the eventual unity of the total cosmos. For in Christ all things hold together.

> He has made known to us the mystery of his will, according to his good pleasure that he set forth in Christ as a plan for the fullness of time, to gather up all things in him, things in heaven and things on earth. (Eph 1:9-10)

In Christ, Christians are called to die to our own narrow dreams and visions in order that we might participate more fully in the fullness of Christ.

2. Centers of Healing and Nurture Within Brokenness and Suffering

Believers in Jesus Christ enter into a new life marked by acceptance and forgiveness. The baptismal waters announce that the past is forgiven; it is buried and cleansed. The believer is given a new identity as a child of God. The child is baptized in Jesus' name (early Christian formulation [Acts 10:48]) or in the name of the Father, Son and Holy Spirit (Matthew 28). One now belongs to God and has a new family name declaring the intrinsic value of every person created by God and of every person for whom Jesus died. The new believer is, and experiences being, reconciled to God and reconciled within God's family. Within this family there is security, a sense of meaning in mission and a hope that disarms the power of death.

The believers, however, continue to be marked by sin and its consequences. Distrust, self-centeredness, disobedience still pervade life. Life is still broken and marked by pain as alienation, guilt, loneliness, irresponsibility, strife, and all the suffering that results from being enmeshed in a sinful world. Lutheran theology speaks of being both sinner and saint, that is, broken and forgiven believer.

Congregations are centers of healing and nurture for broken believers. Christians gather to hear the healing power of the gospel. Forgiveness, comfort, hope, meaning are shared in the reading of Scripture, the preaching of Jesus the Cosmic Crucified, and the celebration of the sacraments. Then there are prayers as the community pours out their gratitude and petitions to God. Prayers are consolation and hope as a people consciously walks and talks with their Cosmic Companion. Then there are hymns of praise; words of encouragement; handclasps and hugs of solidarity as people are fused, healed and empowered by God and God's family.

Healed, nurtured and empowered, the believers leave. They are sent to proclaim that Jesus Christ is Lord and Savior through words and deeds.

3. Centers of Empowered Mission

Emil Brunner wrote, "The church is to mission as fire is to burning."[193] That statement is to be made of every expression of the church, including the congregation. The congregation is to mission as fire is to burning. Each congregation is a center of mission. One of the primary purposes of organizing new congregations is to multiply centers of mission.

The Evangelical Lutheran Church in America/Division for Global Mission's commitments statement reads:

---

[193]Emil Brunner, *The Word and the World* (London: S.C.M. Press, 1931), 108.

Background

Christian congregations are centers of mission. The Holy Spirit through the ministry of Word and Sacrament calls, creates and nurtures ever-new communities of Christians. These persons, empowered by the Holy Spirit, are sent into the world to witness to Jesus Christ. In order that centers of Christian proclamation and witness may be multiplied:

Commitment

We are committed to the planting and growth of new congregations and churches where Christ is not yet known so that Christ might be more widely proclaimed and more fully known. (Commitment 2, "Commitments for Mission in the 1990s")

The Division for Global Mission is deeply committed to organizing new congregations, synods and churches in order that mission might take place. In order to achieve this, the major proportion of all resources are committed to evangelical outreach and to the training of leadership for mission within churches around the world.

In participating in the mission of the body of Christ, it is always essential that the proclamation of the Cosmic Crucified take place in words and in deeds—holistic mission. We noted that Jesus' own mission was holistic, and we have seen how a theology of the cross fuses atonement for sin with actions of and advocacy for righteousness-justice. It is not possible to preach Jesus Christ and ignore service with the poor, oppressed and marginalized in the world. To do so is a denial of the lordship of Jesus Christ.

C. Witnessing Within Cultural Diversity

As the church accompanies the missioning God across geographical, racial, cultural (including linguistic), and faith boundaries, the gospel of Jesus Christ becomes and must become incarnate within new cultural contexts. In order to communicate with the human community, God became human. In order to communicate with specific people, God became incarnate within a specific people. The Son of God was born a specific Jew (of specific Jewish parents), Jesus of Nazareth, who spoke Aramaic, heard and read the ancient Hebrew scriptures and shared their culture and life.

When the early church first moved across cultural and linguistic boundaries, it immediately was aware of the necessity to speak in new languages and to seek for new words and concepts to articulate the meaning of Jesus Christ in that new world. In the incarnation, the one who is in the form of God emptied himself in order to enter the human sphere. Likewise, the missionary church is called to become aware of its enculturation in order that it might become acculturated in a new time and place. In a sense the missionary church is called to continually be emptied of its own cultural forms and values in order that they might bear witness to Christ in the new world into which the church is sent.

The very truth of the gospel of Jesus Christ is in part authenticated by its capacity to become actualized in every historical and cultural situation. The New Testament witnesses to this power of the gospel as it broke out of the ancient and traditional Jewish forms and was articulated within a hellenistic society. The New Testament was written in Greek, not Aramaic, which was the language of Jesus and his disciples. The form and content of the New Testament documents witness to an early church already present and witnessing in a variety of ways within the various contexts of the Roman Empire. Relevance and adaptability to the new missionary situation were a greater priority for the mission of the church than the preservation of a detailed and infallible duplication of the past.

The Nicene Creed, often viewed as a symbol of traditional orthodoxy, actually witnesses to the capacity of the church to empty itself and speak in a new historical and cultural context without denying the reality of God's action in Jesus Christ. The early church exemplifies a missioning church that is a creative, self-emptying people. A static church without capacity to lose its own cultural form is incapable of significant participation in the mission of God.

Effective participation in the mission of the body of Christ is dependent upon the church's willingness to follow the self-emptying Son of God into the world. Once again we are challenged to rethinking mission within a reemphasis upon a theology of the cross, an emphasis on Jesus Christ crucified.

D. Contextualization of the Christian Proclamation

At the heart of the Christian faith and mission is the affirmation that God raised Jesus crucified from the dead. The resurrection of Jesus is God's proclamation that Jesus' message is God's message, that Jesus' mission is God's mission. It is the assertion that God has identified Godself in Jesus and there is no God other than the God revealed in Jesus. Jesus is God's greatest gift to humanity for in, with, and through him we have encountered the mystery in which we live and move and have our being (Acts 17).

The confession of the finality of Jesus for faith in God is the foundation of our Christian mission; however, this fundamental confession has been articulated in various ways within the history of the Christian community. A brief summary of the development of early church confessions will indicate that the lordship of Jesus was from the beginning confessed authentically in a variety of ways. Each confession was an attempt in a new situation to say that God's final and ultimate word had been spoken in Jesus. These confessions make it clear that the church has always been concerned that the confession be both true to Scripture and relevant to the context in which it witnesses.

The New Testament indicates that early statements of faith in Jesus declared that he was a prophet or "the final eschatological prophet." However, within the Jewish community it soon became necessary to describe Jesus as the Messiah in order to claim that it was in Jesus that all the promises of the prophets were fulfilled. However, when early Christianity immediately moved into the hellenistic environment of the Roman Empire, the title messiah was not effective in expressing the faith of the Christian community. In the hellenistic world, where the fulfillment of prophecy in the biblical sense was unknown, the confession that Jesus was the Messiah did not signify that the ultimate revelation of Godself and God's purposes was in Jesus. Hellenism determined ultimate truth and life not in terms of the fulfillment of history but in terms of the presence of the divine. The early Christians were compelled to say that Jesus was the divine embodied among us. Jesus was confessed as the Son of God or the incarnation of the Logos of God. In their world of divine emperors and kings it was absolutely necessary that the one in whom God was ultimately revealed be divine. The New Testament witnesses to these early Christian confessions of Jesus' divinity: "Christ Jesus, who, though he was in the form of God, did not regard equality with God as something to be exploited, but emptied himself, taking the form of a slave, being born in human likeness" (Phil 2:5-7).

Even the confessions of Jesus' divinity did not ultimately suffice within the hellenistic culture, because hellenism allowed for a variety of "divine" agencies and powers, and hellenistic philosophy and theology assumed that above creation and the plethora of divine agencies there was the Ultimate One. Because of its perfection that Ultimate One, source of truth and life, did not and could not be related to creation and history. Some early Christians accepted this hellenistic philosophical principle as ultimate truth. They concluded that the divine incarnate in Jesus was not the Ultimate One but something, although divine, less than the Ultimate God. Therefore, faith in Jesus did not place one in relationship to ultimate truth nor eternal life. The ultimate self-identification of God had not taken place in Jesus.

Others within the early church absolutely refused to accept this conclusion. Their faith forced them to deny and contradict the best philosophical tradition of their day. God, the Ultimate One, was embodied in Jesus. Therefore God could be incarnate in flesh and blood, dust and matter. Faith could affirm that life had been touched with truth and eternity. The hellenistic environment compelled the fourth-century Christians to say at Nicea that in the incarnation, God of God, light of light, God of very God was and is ultimately present and revealed among us.

As Christians we affirm that we are consciously faithful to this tradition in two respects: 1) The finality of Jesus Christ must be maintained in our confession and mission. Jesus Christ the crucified and risen servant is the incarnation of God's presence and action in the world, the Cosmic Crucified. 2) We are also consciously aware, as noted above, that this confession has taken many forms within the history and the traditions of the church. Again and again new situations and contexts call forth new confessions of the Christian faith.

These two presuppositions form the foundation for Christian thinking about the proclamation of the Cosmic Crucified. The one who hung on Calvary has decisive significance for all reality. The discussion has argued that the heart of the universe, God, has defined God's being and mission in this particular Nazarene who in self-giving love was vulnerable unto death. The discussion has also argued that authentic human existence, participating in God's mission in and for the world, is also defined in this same prophetic figure, and therefore all human life and mission is to be conformed to "the one who was rich and became poor." In the Cosmic Crucified is fused the absolute clue to ontological ultimacy and teleological finality.

How that union of God and human destiny in the particularity of Jesus crucified is to be articulated, has taken a multiplicity of forms not only within Christian history but in the New Testament itself.[194]

---

[194]For a recent discussion of this topic, see chapter 5 in Paul Varo Martinson's *A Theology of World Religions* (Minneapolis: Augsburg Publishing, 1987), 215ff.

In an earlier study distributed by the Division for World Mission and Inter-Church Cooperation of the former American Lutheran Church (DWMIC/ALC),[195] it was suggested that within a Muslim world it might be helpful to study and explore the effectiveness of witnessing to God's final word to humanity in terms of Jesus as the crucified and raised prophet. Robert W. Jenson wrote an insightful and creative essay entitled "The Risen Prophet." In it he suggested "that faith's necessary affirmations about Christ can in the Islamic context be made by calling him the 'Risen Prophet.'"[196] Jenson argues that the Nicene confession responded to the question "May not God be different for and in himself" than God appears in Jesus Christ?[197] Arians argued that God was different from Jesus Christ. The Son was only like the Father. God had not ultimately identified Godself in the Son.

The Nicene Creed, in response to various forms of Arianism, stated precisely the opposite, "*that Christ is homousios 'of one being' with 'the Father'*" and therefore God has identified God's own being and future in Jesus Christ. Jenson calls this Nicea's "trinitarian move."[198]

Jenson then continues by suggesting that the same "trinitarian move" might be made within Islam by speaking of Jesus as the "Risen Prophet." The question remains the same, "Might not God be different for and in himself" than what God speaks through the prophet? The fact that God raised Jesus from the dead is God's self-authentication of the prophetic voice of Jesus. God has identified himself in this particular risen prophet. In Nicene terms, this means that the prophetic word is uncreated, belonging to the essential being of God. Jenson notes that Muslims have been open to discussing the nature of the Qur'an in this way.

Finally, Jenson suggests that if Muslims might begin to think of Jesus as the "Risen Prophet," that would not be the end of the discussion. Future Christians within Muslim communities might be driven to ask questions similar to those that engendered the Nicene formulation. How that discussion might be carried on and to what it might lead can only be determined by future Muslims who might possibly be grasped in faith by the Cosmic Crucified.

---

[195]*God and Jesus: Theological Reflections for Christian-Muslim Dialog.* See note 146.

[196]*God and Jesus: Theological Reflections for Christian-Muslim Dialog,* 57.

[197]*God and Jesus: Theological Reflections for Christian-Muslim Dialog,* 63.

[198]*God and Jesus: Theological Reflections for Christian-Muslim Dialog,* 62.

God and Jesus: Theological Reflections for Christian-Muslim Dialog
was developed by DWMIC/ALC as a document to explore possibilities for
the contextualization of theology within the Muslim community. There was
no indication that this was the only or best articulation of the faith within
the Muslim world. It simply argued that it might be effective to speak of
the Cosmic Crucified within the Muslim world in terms of the prophetic
role common to both Muslims and Christians.

There was also no suggestion that the new terminology removed
fundamental differences in how Christians and Muslims understand the
reality of God. The document stated, "The validity of this document does
not depend upon its value in convincing Muslims to be Christians, but in
possibly clarifying for Muslims and Christians how we believe in one God
differently."[199] This discussion has been noted in order to indicate that
even as flexibility and creativity are apparent in the early church's witness
documented in the New Testament, so they are also needed today as
Christians explore how they might witness to the Cosmic Crucified among
people of other faiths.[200]

E. Planning and Implementing for Mission

Acts describes three major missionary journeys of the apostle Paul.
Paul began each of those planned journeys from Antioch, and concluded
two of the three in Antioch. Each journey was planned (Acts 15:36-41);
decisions were made (Acts 16:6-10), and reports were given (Acts 14:27).
Paul and Barnabas's journeys represent the earliest planned mission
expansion of the Christian church. This globe-encircling program was
believed to be firmly rooted in the guidance and power of the Holy Spirit
(Acts 13:1-3; 16:6-10).

Throughout the history of the Christian church there have been
intentional plans made for witnessing to the gospel. The Division for
Global Mission (DGM)/ELCA sees itself within that tradition as it proposes
future directions for its work. An example of the planning carried out by
DGM, under the planning leadership of Dr. Gerald E. Currens, is found in
the following document.

---

[199]*God and Jesus: Theological Reflections for Christian-Muslim Dialog*, 5.

[200]I have made a similar argument for "A Christology of the Spirit" in *Dialog*, 16 (Spring 1977),
135-138.

Major Program Directions 1993

Evangelism

The primary involvement of DGM will be evangelism, specifically a holistic witness among people who have not heard or who have not fully heard the gospel of Jesus Christ.

Our world of five billion people is deeply marred by sin and its consequences. Humanity has turned away from God and insists on walking its own disastrous way. The gospel announces that God, in love sent Jesus Christ into the world as Savior to call for the world's repentance and to die for the sins of the world.

There are two billion people who have not had the opportunity to hear this gospel. Another one and one-half billion persons have a minimal knowledge of Christ. There are, then, three and one-half billion persons who have not had the possibility of responding to God's saving gospel which promises justification by grace through faith in Jesus Christ and new life empowered by the Holy Spirit within the body of Christ.

Therefore, DGM is committed:

To proclaim to those who have not heard or who have not fully heard the gospel that Jesus Christ is Savior and Lord in order that they might believe.

To the planting and growth of new congregations and churches where Christ is not yet known so that Christ may be more widely proclaimed and more fully known.

To send missionaries who know, speak and live out the gospel, and to support the evangelistic efforts and witness of churches with which we cooperate in mission.

Building on its strategic presence within the Muslim world, DGM will make engagement with Muslims a priority.

Islam claims nearly one-fifth of the world's population, a religion second only to the Christian faith in number of adherents. Islam is growing. Muslims are a significant proportion of those who have not heard or—more accurately—not fully heard the gospel of Jesus. And Christians must acknowledge some responsibility over the centuries for this neglected and distorted witness. There is no better time than the present for the development of ministry that will move beyond the mutual misunderstandings of the past.

To do this, DGM is already strategically well placed. To give special emphasis to the world of Islam, DGM can build upon various ministries among Muslims in places where DGM is already engaged: The Middle East, Senegal, Nigeria, Cameroon, Central African Republic, Madagascar, Ethiopia, India, Indonesia and England. Furthermore, with many Muslims now living in Europe and North America, greater engagement with Muslims is already, in one way or another, a reality for many members of the ELCA.

In giving work among Muslims a special emphasis and focus, DGM will:

a. First, adequately staff and fund present programs where there is contact with Muslim communities.

b. More adequately prepare present and future DGM missionaries for interfaith conversations and witness among Muslims.

c. Support among partner churches and others programs of research, dialogue and witness and offer opportunities to better equip personnel for witness among Muslims.

d. Take advantage of the skills and experience of specialists in Islam for the preparation of DGM personnel and others for engagement with Muslims both in the U.S. and abroad.

e. Enter new areas of the Muslim world as funding becomes available, based upon a comprehensive plan for DGM's priority and special emphasis on Islam.

Building upon its presence and strength, DGM will give priority to witness within the world of Buddhism and secularism in Asia.

In adopting evangelism as a priority (March 1990), the DGM board asserted that "DGM will further develop expertise in the study of and encounter with Buddhism and secularism as they both develop in modern Asia." This priority is consistent with DGM's long-range goal of sharing the good news of Jesus Christ "with those who acknowledge no faith, people of other faiths and adherents of various ideologies."

As a result of historic ties with some churches as well as more recent and still developing relationships, DGM already has invaluable resources to draw upon in the knowledge and experience of Christians within Asia and their encounter with various schools of Buddhism, with folk religion and secularism. Through our relationships with churches in Thailand, Singapore, Malaysia, Hong Kong, Taiwan, Japan, and the Christian community in China, DGM can with them develop this witness within modern Asia.

To implement this priority of witness within the world of Buddhism and secularism in Asia, DGM will:

a. Evaluate present programs and involvement in the light of this priority and, where presently effective or having a potential for the future, will strengthen DGM's involvement.

b. Develop expertise among DGM missionaries in Asian culture, with a specific focus on Buddhism, popular folk religion and secularism in the Asian context.

c. Learn from the experience of Christians in Asia in their witness to Buddhists and secularists.

d. Support among partner churches and others programs of research, dialogue and witness and offer opportunities to better equip personnel for witness within the contexts of Buddhism, popular folk religion and secularism.

e. Explore new initiatives, in consultation and cooperation with Lutheran churches and other church bodies and ecumenical organizations, and as funding becomes available.

Cooperation

Building upon its long standing relationships with many churches around the world, DGM will give primary emphasis to efforts that enhance interdependence and mutuality in mission, thereby lessening dependence upon DGM funding and personnel.

With the formation of the ELCA, the DGM legacy from predecessor church bodies and previous Lutheran mergers was relationships with twenty-one churches with which this church has historical ties. These are churches which missionaries of predecessor church bodies had a role in establishing or in which a sizeable number of missionaries from predecessor church bodies have served over a significant number of years. Some of these shared histories span three, four and five generations.

These connections with partner churches are long and deep; they have also evolved over the years. Yet for some—not all—of these churches, relationships with DGM and their European mission partners are colored by a persistent and pervasive dependence upon funds and personnel from abroad. This deprives the church and its partners of mutuality in mission and fuller expressions of interdependence. For DGM, this ongoing dependency ties up limited resources in programs of institutional maintenance.

In addition to partner churches and international congregations with historical ties to the ELCA and its predecessor bodies, DGM has inherited or developed more recent church to church relationships that are also more fully interdependent. Under the auspices of the Lutheran World Federation, the opportunity has opened up for special relationships between the ELCA and such Lutheran churches as those in Eastern and Central Europe, the small Evangelical Church of the Lutheran Confession in Cuba, and the Lutheran Church in the Philippines. Mutuality and interdependence can be more fully realized within the communion of churches that is the Lutheran World Federation.

The move from patterns of dependency to a mutual sharing of gifts and resources between the ELCA and churches with which we cooperate can have considerable impact upon the way DGM's resources are allocated in the future.

A key strategy will be even more focus upon leadership development.

DGM will emphasize contextual, formal and informal ways to enable persons to learn, grow and be equipped and empowered to give leadership in the living out of the gospel in their churches, communities and societies.

a. DGM will give priority to programs that develop the potential and leadership of women, including the literacy, basic education and training prerequisite to reaching their full human potential and to achieving full participation in decision-making in church and society. Recognizing that the church must challenge cultural assumptions as to the normativeness of male models of organizing and interpreting human experience, DGM, in its program planning and implementation, will give voice to, and incorporate programmatic expression of, alternative models based on women's experience, wisdom and gifts.

b. DGM will focus on programs of theological education and support programs that strengthen the ministry of both lay and ordained persons.

c. DGM will send missionaries who will equip and empower others for leadership.

d. DGM will encourage and empower leadership development for churches in the southern hemisphere that will effectively meet the local and regional, present and future needs of these churches.

Such a sharpened focus upon interdependence, financial self-sufficiency, leadership and empowerment will mean, among other things:

a. For some partner churches, a shift by DGM from (1) supporting church administration and institutions, (2) subsidizing congregational life or pastors' salaries, or (3) assigning missionary pastors who will serve primarily established congregations.

b. A change in thinking from the number of missionary positions to which a partner church is entitled to an assessment of how a missionary contributes, for example, to leadership formation, empowerment of women, or engagement with persons who have not heard the good news of Jesus Christ.

c. Encouraging international English-speaking congregations in Europe and elsewhere and congregations serving the U.S. military to become financially self-sufficient; or finding ways for the costs of such congregations to be shared among ecumenical partners.

d. Moving from maintenance of those relationships in South America that are largely traditional church cooperation to finding creative ways to undergird evangelism, promote solidarity with poor and oppressed people and empower local leadership. There will be an overall reduction in grants and long-term personnel in South America.

South-South Relationships

This century has witnessed the astounding growth of the Christian church in areas of the world beyond Europe and North America. DGM has chosen as a major program direction the developing, facilitating and nurturing of exchanges, relationships, cooperation and mutual involvement in mission among churches of the southern hemisphere–Africa, the Middle East, Asia, and Latin America.

a. DGM will encourage and empower cooperation among churches in the southern hemisphere by helping them to engage in bilateral and multilateral conferences, to identify common problems and to search for effective solutions.

b. DGM will encourage the development and exchange of leaders among churches of the South, a sharing of experience and insights into the Christian faith that will affirm and enhance the ministry and mission of these churches.

c. DGM will cooperate with the LWF [Lutheran World Federation] and other ecumenical agencies to identify, inventory and encourage the sharing of appropriate resources among churches in the south and between churches in the south and those of the north.

Poverty and Oppression

Within the scope of God's mission to this world, those who suffer from poverty and oppression have a special claim upon the concern, commitment and resources of the ELCA.

a.   In view of the massive poverty in the world, DGM will put resources where they are most needed.

b.   DGM will give special emphasis to advocacy on behalf of those without voice, influence or power, for example, women and children. DGM will participate in the ELCA's specific focus on women and children at risk.

c.   DGM will support efforts that accompany and empower poor and oppressed people.

Mission to the ELCA

The DGM education program will work to increase the concern and the involvement of every member and every congregation in Christ's mission to the world: expanding awareness, renewing prayer life and increasing support for the ELCA global mission program. The primary methodology will be strategies that enable ELCA members to receive and experience the gifts and witness of members of churches with whom the ELCA cooperates.

a.   DGM will give priority to establishing and supporting Companion Synod relationships between ELCA synods and congregations and the churches overseas.

b.   DGM will give priority to developing networks of congregational and synod leaders equipped to motivate and educate ELCA members for participation in global mission programs. Within this program, DGM will develop special strategies for working with ELCA youth and the African American, Asian American, Hispanic and Native American communities.

c.   DGM will give priority to conducting, with synods and other ELCA units, three Global Mission Events annually, giving focus to education for mission locally and globally.

d.   DGM will give priority to developing networks of congregations and members who support the ELCA global mission program through financial commitments through the proportionate share with synods, the Missionary Sponsorship program and designated gifts.

e.   DGM will give priority to developing strategies that equip ELCA members for interfaith conversations and witness with Muslims.

F.　Final Comment

"But you will receive power when the Holy Spirit has come upon you; and you will be my witnesses . . . and to the ends of the earth." (Acts 1:8)

Jesus' words are a declaration: "You will receive power; you will be my witnesses." This is a declaration of a future approaching reality. It is a God-given reality consisting of Jesus Christ and the Holy Spirit. Jesus Christ will have witnesses. The Holy Spirit will embolden the timid and fearful that they may witness powerfully to that one who for our sins hung on Calvary dying in the darkness, dust and wind. The emboldened in the presence of danger and death will testify that the crucified Jesus is raised, lives, and sits at the right hand of God.

We will be empowered witnesses to that! Within this context we hear Jesus' imperative:

"Go therefore and make disciples of all nations, baptizing them in the name of the Father and of the Son and of the Holy Spirit, and teaching them to obey everything that I have commanded you. And remember, I am with you always, to the end of the age." (Mt 28:19-20)

Appendix 1
CHRISTIAN AND MUSLIM UNDERSTANDINGS OF REVELATION

[This paper was prepared in the early 1960s by Mark Thomsen for students of the Theological College of Northern Nigeria. Revised July 1992 to reflect more inclusive language.]

The Bible contains and proclaims the prophetic and apostolic faith through which God speaks to God's people. In what way does God speak to the prophets and apostles, and in what way does God speaks through them? Since the Bible contains and proclaims the faith and message which we are seeking to understand, we must begin by asking ourselves what kind of book is the Bible for if we can determine the nature of the Bible we will have learned a great deal about its faith and message.

1. The Islamic View of Revelation and the Qur'an

In the attempt to understand what type of book the Bible is, it will be very helpful if we compare the Bible with the Muslim beliefs concerning the scriptures of the Islamic faith, the Qur'an. This comparison will show us very clearly a number of things concerning the nature of the Bible, and we will find that our understanding of the Bible as Christians is different from the Muslim understanding of the Qur'an. It is true that the Christian believes that God speaks through the Bible, and the Muslim believes that God speaks through the Qur'an but the way in which Christians and Muslims understand this speaking of God is very different.

The Muslim has a very simple understanding of the Qur'an as the Word of God, and therefore a very simple understanding of revelation. The Muslim believes that God speaks to prophets, giving them a message which is verbally passed on to the people. Thus God speaks to the people by the prophets. The Muslim believes that there have been many prophets, among whom are Abraham, Moses, and Jesus, but the last and final prophet is Muhammad. God, in a series of revelations, spoke verbally to Muhammad. These revelations were collected and form the Qur'an. The Qur'an is literally God's verbal word. These are the words which came from heaven and words which Muhammad heard. Furthermore, God's word came to Muhammad in Arabic, and thus only the Arabic Qur'an is God's word for God did not speak in Hausa or English. Thus any translation of the Qur'an is not called God's word but an interpretation, for the translation no longer contains the original word spoken by God. This briefly is the Muslim understanding of revelation and the sacred book of Islam, the Qur'an.

The Muslim understanding of the Qur'an is found in the Qur'an itself. In a number of passages we read that Muhammad was given his heavenly message, and at times it is said that this message was brought to him from God by an angel. In Surah 75:16 we read that Muhammad received instructions to listen carefully to the heavenly message before speaking it himself: "Move not thy tongue in haste to follow and master this revelation, for we will see to the collecting and recital [reading, is found in the translation by Pickthall] of it; but when we have recited [read] it, then follow the recital [reading]." In Surah 53:1ff we read that Muhammad does not err nor is he deceived, for the message which he proclaims is given to him by a heavenly messenger.

> By the star when it setteth. Your comrade erreth not, nor is deceived; . . . It is naught save an inspiration that is inspired.[1]

This Muslim view of revelation is briefly summarized by Nasum Saifi, Chief Ahmadiyya missionary to West Africa: "Of course He [Allah] talks to His chosen ones and gives them His commandments to be conveyed to other human beings. That is the kind of revelation which has always been taking place."[2] In summary, Islamic theology asserts that revelation is the message of God given to a prophet in order that it might be proclaimed to the world.

This concept of revelation is found not only in Islam but also in numerous religions of the world, including African traditional religion. K. A. Busia, writing on the religion of the Ashanti people of West Africa, states that "the spirit of the god speaks through his priest, sometimes by displacing the personality of the priest, so that he becomes a mere medium behaving and speaking as compelled by the spirit that possesses him."[3]

---

[1]*The Glorious Qur'an*, trans. Muhammad M. Pickthall (1953; reprint, New York: New American Library of World Literature, 1960), Surah 53:1-12.

[2]Nasum Saifi, *Presenting Islam to the Christians* (Lagos: Chief Ahmadiyya Bookshop, 1961), 32.

[3]Daryll Forde, ed. *African Worlds* (London: Oxford University Press, 1964), 194.

This idea of revelation has also greatly influenced the thought of many Jewish and Christian writers. A striking example is related in the fourteenth chapter of 2 Esdras (IV Ezra), a book contained in some texts of the Old Testament Apocrypha.[4] In this book it is related that God's law (the Old Testament) had been burned and the people no longer knew what God had done or would do. Therefore, Ezra asks, "If then I have found favour beside thee, send the Holy Spirit into me and I will write everything that has happened in the world from the beginning, the things which were written in thy law, that men may be able to find the path" (2 Esdras 14:22). Ezra's prayer is answered favorably, and he is told to employ five secretaries who could write rapidly.

> And on the next day, behold, a voice called me saying, "Ezra, open your mouth and drink what I give you to drink." Then I opened my mouth, and behold, a full cup was offered to me; it was full of something like water, but its colour was like fire. And I took it and drank; and when I had drunk it, my heart poured forth understanding, and wisdom increased in my breast, for my spirit retained its memory; and my mouth was opened, and was no longer closed. And the Most High gave understanding to the five men, and by turns they wrote what was *dictated*, in characters which they did not know. They sat forty days, and wrote during the daytime, and ate their bread at night. As for me, I spoke in the daytime and was not silent at night. So during the forty days ninety-four books were written. (Esdras 14:38-44)

These examples reveal that the view of revelation accepted by Islam is widely found in the world's religions. Therefore, one cannot accept the claim that Islam, Christianity, or any other religion is the final revealed religion just because Muhammad or some other prophet said God spoke to him. Other people and prophets have claimed the same authority, and therefore, the manner or the means by which it is claimed that the heavenly message was received cannot prove the truth of the message.

---

[4]The Old Testament Apocrypha is considered by Protestant Christians to stand outside the Canonical or Authoritative scriptures; however, they are accepted as Canonical by the Roman Catholic Church.

2. *A Christian-Muslim Conversation Concerning the Bible*

We now have some understanding of the Muslim view of revelation. With this knowledge let us now in our imagination carry on a conversation with a Muslim friend who has this direct, simple understanding of the Word of God.   This will help us to understand the nature of the Bible itself.

To make a favorable impression on Ahmadu, our Muslim friend, we will first take him to the book of Jeremiah 7:1. There we read,

> The word that came to Jeremiah from the Lord: "Stand in the gate of the Lord's house, and proclaim there this word, and say, Hear the word of the Lord. Thus says the Lord of hosts, the God of Israel, Amend your ways and your doings, and I will let you dwell in this place."

Our Muslim friend has no difficulty understanding what we mean when we say that this is God's word. Jeremiah may not be known to him, but he can immediately see that Jeremiah was a prophet of God. He was a prophet for he received a verbal message from God and he, in turn, proclaimed that message to his people, Israel. However, while paging through the rest of the book of Jeremiah, Ahmadu's eye falls upon a passage in chapter 20: "O Lord, thou hast deceived me" and further down the page, "Cursed be the day on which I was born." Immediately we are questioned, "Who speaks this blasphemy?" We reply that it is a prayer of Jeremiah, and we suggest that it would be helpful to read the whole chapter in order to understand Jeremiah's thoughts and feelings. Our study reveals that Jeremiah, because of his God-given message, has daily faced ridicule and persecution. Because Jeremiah is a very sensitive man he inwardly suffers as he sees himself and his message denounced by his own people. In despair he cries out to God, "Cursed be the day on which I was born." Ahmadu says that he understands Jeremiah's thought, but he does not understand how this can possibly be God's word. Ahmadu continues, "This is not a message spoken by God to his prophet which is to be proclaimed to God's people. This is rather a prayer of a suffering man as he cries out to God. Would it not be correct to take this passage out of your Bible since it is not God's word?"

Perhaps this question strikes us as rather strange but from Ahmadu's understanding of revelation it is quite logical. If revelation is limited to God's verbally given message, why should the word of God include the prayers of people? For the present we reply to Ahmadu that God speaks not only by the prophets but he speaks *through* the prophets. As we read Jeremiah's messages we hear God speak to us, but also, as we read of his faith and his experiences, God speaks *through* this faith and these experiences to us. The faith and lives of the prophets as well as their messages become God's word, for God speaks through the lives and words of his servants. Tremendous spiritual power is added to the message of Hosea because we learn of the tragedy of his marriage; the message of Jonah becomes alive in the context of Jonah's refusal to obey the will of God. God speaks through these persons because God has been in their lives as well as in their message. Ahmadu quietly says, "The Bible seems to be a very human book." "Yes," we reply, "a very human book, but if the Bible is God's word it means that God has been in our world. He has been in the lives of people."

From the prophets we take Ahmadu to the historical writings of the Old Testament. Ahmadu was surprised by Jeremiah, but he is shocked by Samuel and Kings. "How can this possibly be considered to be God's Word? This is the history of the nation of Israel. Therefore, it certainly cannot be God's word unless perhaps God dictated this history from heaven." We could save ourselves a good deal of patient explanation if we would accept the message of 2 Esdras and just say to Ahmadu, "Yes, this history was dictated from heaven," but we would not be honestly interpreting the Bible nor would we give Ahmadu a true understanding of how these books stand as part of God's word. So instead of seeking an easy answer we will try to give a meaningful explanation. We begin by stating that these books are a part of God's word, but we add that they were not dictated from heaven. The prophets who wrote the history of Israel were men who relied upon ancient historical records for information which they did not witness themselves. Without confusing Ahmadu with a great deal of information set forth by recent Old Testament scholars, we indicate to him that the writer of Joshua used an ancient book called the Book of Jashar (Jos 10:13); the writer of Numbers quoted from the Book of the Wars of the Lord (Nm 21:14); the writer of Chronicles had read the Chronicles of Samuel the Seer, the Chronicles of Nathan the Prophet, and the Chronicles of Gad the Seer (1 Chr 29:29). These few examples convince Ahmadu that we do not think that these books were dictated from heaven. But this then leads Ahmadu in exasperation to ask, "How then *do* you consider these books to be a portion of God's revelation?"

We state simply that God was at work in the history of Israel, and that the prophets had been led by God to see that God was indeed present and active among God's people. The so-called history books of the Old Testament are not primarily interested in the activities of Israel, but rather in the activities of God. These books tell the story of God's work within Israel. This activity of God was not seen by all persons, but it was seen by the prophets who through faith saw God's work. For example, 2 Kings records the destruction of Jerusalem, and according to the book of Kings the destruction of Jerusalem was the direct result of God's judgment falling upon a disobedient people. Most of the populace of ancient Judah did not understand the city's destruction in this way. Some thought that King Zedekiah had been a political fool in attempting to rebel against the armed might of Babylon, while many cursed Egypt for failing to effectively support the revolt, and others just cursed. But in and through this national tragedy, the prophets saw the mighty arm of God. It was God who destroyed Jerusalem, and Nebuchadnezzar was but a tool in his hand. It is because the prophetic writers through faith saw God in Israel's history that these books form a portion of God's word. God spoke through the historical experiences of Israel, for, according to the prophets, God was in those experiences. The historical books bear witness to this activity of God seen by the prophets, and through these events God is known not only to Israel but to us, who, through these books, are made witnesses of these same mighty acts of God. Ahmadu thinks a moment, then says, "It is a different understanding of revelation than I have." "But, if it is true," we reply, "it means that God has been at work among these people in a very wonderful way. God has been in the historical events of Israel's history, and God has also been in the lives of the prophets, opening their eyes, or, in other words, giving them faith to see the divine work which was being accomplished in the midst of them."

As we page past the historical books of the Old Testament, Ahmadu notices the Book of Psalms and asks, "What are the Psalms?" We answer that they are a collection of prayers and songs used by the people of Israel in their worship of God. Ahmadu smiles and says, "Your Bible becomes more strange all the time. Now you tell me that God's word even includes a hymn and prayer book." Yes, it even includes a hymn book. The Psalms are a collection of Israel's hymns and prayers which were sung in response to God's acts of love and salvation. Through these hymns God's acts are proclaimed; through these hymns we see godly people give thanks and praise to God; through these hymns we see people who earnestly confess their sins and seek for fellowship with God; and thus through these hymns God speaks to us concerning God's grace and God calls us to respond even as did the Israelites of old. Ahmadu says, "It is a very human book." "Yes," we reply," and if true, God has been in the lives of these people, moving them outwardly and inwardly through these songs of praise, confession, supplication, and thanksgiving." With that Ahmadu begins to read from Psalm 30.

To thee, O Lord, I cried; and to the Lord I made supplication: "What profit is there in my death, if I go down to the Pit? Will the dust praise thee? Will it tell of thy faithfulness? Hear, O God, and be gracious to me! O Lord, be thou my helper!"

Thou hast turned for me my mourning into dancing; thou has loosed my sackcloth and girded me with gladness that my soul may praise thee and not be silent. O Lord my God, I will give thanks to thee forever.

"Beautiful and powerful," says Ahmadu. "The psalmist knew the meaning of praise and thanksgiving." Ahmadu sits in thought and then with an inquisitive look asks, "Don't you Christians believe in the resurrection of the dead?"

"Certainly," we reply. "It is one of the central teachings of the New Testament." But Ahmadu answers that he doesn't believe this psalmist had this hope of resurrection, for he gives thanks that God has saved him from death, thus making it possible for him to praise God. Furthermore, he states that if he had died he would not have been able to praise God. This psalmist has no hope for life after death.

The thought flashed through our mind that it would have been much easier if Ahmadu had chosen to read Psalm 23, but he has read Psalm 30 and perhaps it is better, for now we can show him how God has bound himself to real people. God speaks through the lives of people who share the thoughts of those round them, and for this we thank God. If it were not true we would have never understood God. With this in mind we begin our explanation to Ahmadu. We explain that the ancient Israelites were Semitic peoples and that among these ancient people there was really no hope of true life after death. They believed that after death all persons descended to a realm beneath the earth called Sheol. This was a dismal and hopeless world for there was no work, or thought or knowledge or wisdom there. A number of passages in the Old Testament reveal that the Israelites tended to share this view (Eccl 9:1-10, Job 10:20-22). God thus came to a people having these thoughts; God relates to a people having human limitations, and God spoke to this people and through this people. As the people listened they came more fully to understand God's plan for creation. Thus in later prophetic passages of the Old testament the hope of the resurrection springs forth and is proclaimed   (Is 26:19, Dn 12:2), and in the New Testament it becomes a reality with the resurrection of Christ, the first fruits of those who have fallen asleep (1 Cor 15:20). This time we say, "It is a very human book, Ahmadu, and it means that God has stooped down to work in our world; God has bound

Godself to humanity limited in knowledge just as you and I; and God has chosen to speak to such people and through such persons. It means that God has been in our world; God has walked through our world and people have met God and come to know God." As Ahmadu ponders this thought, we turn our Bible to the New Testament.

We want lastly to speak to Ahmadu about the Gospels, so now we turn to the letters of Paul and the other apostles. "This book has no end of surprises," remarks Ahmadu, "even letters. What is the purpose of them?" We explain that there are a number of letters in the New Testament written by various men to various churches. They are written to these churches on specific occasions in order to instruct, exhort and correct. As an example we give a brief account of 1 Corinthian. We explain that the Corinthian church was literally in a mess. There were divisions within the church, legal disputes and immorality; there were problems concerning marriage, food offered to idols, sacramentalism; drunkenness at worship services; there were conflicts concerning spiritual gifts and the resurrection from the dead; and finally there was the collection of money for the saints in Jerusalem. In this one letter Paul attempts to bring some Christian obedience and order to the church at Corinth by writing concerning each of these problems. This letter has been included in God's word because it gives an apostle's God-inspired instructions concerning the Christian faith and life. "I see," says Ahmadu, "these words of inspired instruction are understood as God's word because God gave these words to Paul from heaven in the same way as our prophet Muhammad received the Qur'an." Again we wish that we could just agree with Ahmadu, but there immediately comes to our mind a passage from   1 Corinthians 7: "A wife is bound to her husband as long as he lives. If the husband dies, she is free to be married to whom she wishes, only in the Lord. But in my judgement she is happier if she remains as she is, And I think that I have the spirit of God" (vss 39-40). As we read the passage to Ahmadu he smiles and says, "This certainly doesn't sound like Muhammad. Muhammad in the Qur'an never speaks about my judgment, he rather proclaims God's judgment. Muhammad doesn't say 'I think I have the spirit of God' but rather 'God said.'" "Very true," we reply, "but the church believes that Paul was led by the Spirit of God, and if it is true that Paul does proclaim a message of God, it means that God was at work in the heart and mind of Paul. God did not shout from heaven, but rather entered the life of Paul and spoke through him to his church. Furthermore, we add, "Paul usually speaks with a power and an authority which will rival the authoritative note of Muhammad himself. However, Paul does not find this authoritative message in a voice from heaven but rather in the life, death and resurrection of Jesus Christ."

We have now brought Ahmadu to the very heart of the apostolic faith and message. The apostles' proclamation was the proclamation that God had made Jesus of Nazareth Christ and Lord. The New Testament makes it very clear that all Jews did not accept this message, but God through the Holy Spirit had opened the eyes of the apostles so that in faith they saw that God was at work in Jesus whom they believed God had made Messiah and Lord. This is the message which the New Testament contains and proclaims concerning Jesus. It is the apostolic message of faith, and it is through this faith, and message that God has worked and still works among us.

As we spoke of Jesus, a knowing look came to Ahmadu's face. He has heard of Jesus: He is a prophet, a very famous prophet, and so with great anticipation Ahmadu turns with us to the Gospels. However, Ahmadu is immediately disturbed for he sees not one Gospel but four Gospels. He explains to us what he has been taught concerning the gospel. As a Muslim he believes that Jesus is a great prophet of the Jews who received a message from God, and that message is called "the gospel". "Now," says Ahmadu, "how is it possible that Jesus received four different messages from God? This only proves that we Muslims are correct when we say that you Christians have lost and perverted the true gospel."

At once we realize that Ahmadu completely misunderstands what we mean by "the gospel." To begin with, the gospel is not just the message of Jesus, for the gospel proclaims both the life and message of Jesus. We explain to Ahmadu that the gospel is not just a collection of the messages of Jesus, but the Gospels are filled with stories about the life and work of Jesus. Ahmadu has by now ceased being surprised, but he cannot help but ask, "Why do you Christians consider the life of Jesus to be so important? Is not the message of Jesus from God, the very Word of God, more important that the story of Jesus, the prophet?"

A million things run through our mind which we would like to tell Ahmadu about Jesus. But how best can we tell him what Jesus means to us as Christians? It would be useless to start by telling him that we believe that Jesus is the Son of God. From the Qur'an, Ahmadu has learned to reject completely the "Christian" thought that God physically begets a Son. He has also been taught that God is one and that the "Christian" idea of three Gods (Father, Jesus, and his mother Mary) is to be rejected as complete blasphemy. We could begin by explaining that the Muslim has misunderstood what the Christian means when he talks of Jesus as the Son of God, or when he talks of the Trinity. Such a discussion would take perhaps hours before it would lead Ahmadu to the slightest understanding of what Jesus means to us. Perhaps we can find a more profitable way of speaking of Jesus. Ahmadu's interest lies in the word of God. Let us attempt to start here. The New Testament faith proclaims that Jesus is the incarnation of God's word. Furthermore, The Qur'an vaguely speaks of Jesus as the word of God (Surah 3:45, 4:171). With this in mind and with a prayer in our hearts we address Ahmadu.

"Ahmadu, as Christians we believe that God speaks to us through the message of Jesus, but we believe that God speaks even more powerfully through the life of Jesus. We have already said that God speaks through the lives of prophets, apostles and other biblical personalities but we believe that God has spoken more fully through the life of Jesus. In fact, we believe that God has fully revealed Godself to us through this person. This is possible because God was bound completely to this person, and this person has bound himself completely to God. God thus speaks through Jesus, for Jesus' words and actions are an expression of the heart and will of God. As Christians we call this the incarnation, by which we mean that the Word of God became Jesus, and thus Jesus was the means whereby the Word of God was experienced by humanity. In the words of the Gospel of John, "the Word became flesh and dwelt among us" (Jn 1:14). When the Christians hear Jesus' message of the kingdom of heaven, they believe that they hear God's message; when they see Jesus seek out sinners, outcasts and harlots, they believe that they see God search for people; when they watch Jesus struggle in prayer in the Garden of Gethsemane, they believe they see God powerfully seeking to have his will done upon this earth. When they see Jesus rise to meet his betrayer, the Christian believes that God who was bound to Jesus is having his will carried out in Jesus. When they see nails driven into the hands and feet of Jesus and when they hear Jesus say, 'Father forgive them,' they believe that they see the very heart of God laid open before them. Jesus' message is God's message; his work is God's work; his love is God's love; his suffering is God's suffering.

"Is it possible," says Ahmadu, "that God, the holy God should bind himself in this way to the weakness of human flesh? Does God condescend to speak through suffering, through a criminal death—the cross?" As we ponder Ahmadu's question, we remember that the cross, the suffering, and the weakness have always raised this question. It was a stumbling block to the Jews and foolishness to the Gentiles, for it always brought one thought to mind "Oh, the weakness of God." Yes, in Christ we see the weakness of God, for God has stooped to bind Godself to our world to our history, to our humanity. God is bound to us and thus God is always Immanuel, God is with us. With this overwhelming thought in mind, we answer Ahmadu: "Yes, we believe that God has spoken through weakness, through suffering, through a cross, for we believe that God was bound to Jesus." "This means then," replies Ahmadu, "that to you Jesus is more than a prophet. A prophet proclaims God's word, but Jesus is God's word. It means that I must not only seek for Jesus' message, but I must seek Jesus himself, for if I have seen him I have seen the very heart and mind of God." Exactly Ahmadu, exactly.

"But if you have this perfect revelation of God in Jesus, why don't you study the gospel and throw the rest of your Bible away?" questions Ahmadu. That's a good question, Ahmadu, and others have suggested something similar. But you see, Ahmadu, Jesus is the climax to the very special work of God in our world; Jesus worshiped and served the God of Abraham, Isaac, and Jacob; Jesus came to fulfill a plan of salvation which God had begun many centuries earlier through Abraham. We cannot really understand God's final Word to humanity unless we see Jesus as a part of this story. Furthermore, according to the whole New Testament that story is not yet complete. The story continues today, for the work of God continues in and through the people that Jesus has called to be his people, the church. God in Jesus began a work of reconciliation; that means that Jesus began a work whereby humanity is called back from sin into fellowship with God. That work is not ended. Millions in every generation live in separation from God. God's people, called together by Jesus Christ, carry on this work of Jesus today, seeking sinners as Jesus did, loving and serving people as he did, suffering with and for them as Jesus did, reconciling sinners as he did. As truly as God was at work in Jesus, God is also at work in and through Jesus' people. God is forever Immanuel; God is forever God with us. Because I believe that God was speaking *through* the prophets and *in* Jesus, I believe that God has been in our world and is still in our world. The Bible is a very human book, Ahmadu, but for this we give thanks and praise to God, for it means that God has been and is very near to us. It means that God is in our world; it means that God has walked and is walking through our world and people have met God here and have come to know him. It means, Ahmadu, that we too can meet God here and we, too, can come to know him. We can learn to rise every morning and call God "Father"; and thus, through Jesus, become the children of God. This is our faith Ahmadu, and we believe that it is an unconquerable faith, for we believe that God raised Jesus from the dead, proclaiming to us who follow him that no power, not even death, shall prevent God's Word from accomplishing that which God sends it forth to do (Is 55:10-11)."

3. Reflections on the Christian-Muslim Conversation

Thinking back over the previous conversation, we are able to make a number of general statements which are true concerning the means of Biblical revelation:

1. The Bible is not one book, nor is it one type of literature, but rather, it is a it is a collection of various types of writings, all of which bear witness to the prophetic-apostolic faith. However, some of these books give a much clearer and fuller witness to this faith than do other biblical books. For example, in the Old Testament the book of Isaiah bears a much fuller witness to the prophetic faith and message than does the Book of Esther, and within the New Testament the Gospel of Luke bears a much fuller witness to the apostolic faith than does the third Letter of John.

2. The heart or we might say the back-bone of the biblical revelation is given through what we sometimes call the "acts of God." This means that God and God's will are revealed through events, through happenings. The best examples of this type of revelation are the Exodus, through which God's electing love is revealed to Israel; the destruction of Jerusalem, through which God revealed judgement of sin; the return from exile, through which God reveals perseverance in seeking salvation for all people; the life, death and resurrection of Jesus, through which God's love and purpose for the world is revealed. These were happenings which took place within the history of the Hebrew people, and through these happenings God has spoken and revealed himself.

3. We have said that revelation takes place in the Bible through events, but these events by themselves do not make revelation. In order that revelation takes place, these events must be seen, interpreted and understood in a certain way. We sometimes say that they must be seen by the eyes of faith. An illustration of this was noted above when it was mentioned that not all the citizens of Jerusalem saw its destruction as a judgement of God upon the nation of Israel. However, the prophets, led by the Spirit of God, saw the hand of God in this event. Again, not all people saw God at work in Jesus, who is proclaimed by faith to be the Messiah. In fact, many of his enemies claimed that he performed his mighty works by the power of Satan. However, the apostles were led by the Spirit of God to see God in Jesus' life and work. After Peter confessed that Jesus was the Christ, Matthew records the following words of Jesus: "Blessed are you, Simon Bar Jona! For flesh and blood has not revealed this to you but my Father who is in Heaven" (Mt 16:17). Thus, revelation takes place when God's mighty acts are seen by eyes of faith

which have been opened by the Spirit of God. The opening of the eyes of faith by the Spirit of God is one aspect of inspiration. The word inspiration means literally to breathe into, and when we use the word in theology, we mean that the Spirit of God enters into the lives of people and works in them. The result of that inner working of God's Spirit is that peoples' eyes are opened to see God's work in Israel and in Jesus who is proclaimed Christ.

Thus in summary we can say that the backbone of revelation is Deed-Word revelation. That is, revelation takes place when a mighty act of God is witnessed and understood or interpreted by a prophet, apostle, or person of God who has been given eyes of faith by the Spirit of God.

4. One of the "acts of God" witnessed to in the Bible is the prophetic word, that is, God is speaking to the prophets of Israel, giving them his Word to be proclaimed to God's people. In Amos we read:

> Then Amos answered Amaziah, "I am no prophet, nor a prophet's son; but I am a herdsman, and a dresser of sycamore trees, and the Lord took me from following the flock, and Lord said to me, "Go, prophesy to my people Israel." Now therefore hear the word of the Lord. (Am 7:14-16)

In Jeremiah we read, "Then the Lord put forth his hand and touched my mouth; and the Lord said to me, 'Behold, I have put my words in your mouth'"(Jer 1:9). Because God gave his message to the prophets they were able to interpret the events in which God was acting; they were also able to proclaim what was the will of God for the people, and finally they were at times led to speak of events before they occurred. Amos, Hosea, Jeremiah, and Ezekiel saw the coming destruction of their nation before the armies of destruction appeared. Thus the prophets were not only men who proclaimed the word of God, but they were men who saw in advance God's coming judgment or salvation and in the light of this knowledge proclaimed a message either of warning or of comfort. Perhaps then it would be better if we would not speak simply of deed-word revelation, but rather of word-deed-word revelation.

5. The prophetic-word plays a central role in biblical revelation. However, the Biblical message proclaims that the final revelation of God was not contained within the words of a prophet. The final revelation of God was a revelation which no prophetic word could contain, for it was given through the life, death, and resurrection of a person, Jesus of Nazareth. The Christian faith declares that God is personal and that this personal God has been revealed in this world through a person. Christians

give thanks to God for this full revelation and believe it to be very fitting for the personal God to be revealed through a person. At this point, the Christian view of revelation is very different from the Islamic view. Naseem Saifi writes, "He [Allah] does not reveal himself in the shape of a human being, because a human being can never have the attributes of God in full force. *The revelation of God in the form of a person therefore never takes place.*"[5] On the contrary, the Christian believes that God's final revelation did take place through a person, and the fullness of that revelation could never have been contained in a prophetic word. Christians, in the words of the book of Hebrews, give thanks to God that they can say, "In many and various ways God spoke of old to our fathers by the prophets; but in these last days he has spoken to us through a Son" (Heb 1:1-2).

At the same time as we say that God's final revelation has come through a person, we must also say that the revelation of God in the Old Testament already prepares the way for this final revelation. We say this because we have seen in our previous conversation that the revelation of God in the Old Testament is not limited to the prophetic word. Already in the Old Testament we see God acting and inspiring the lives of faithful prophets; and as God works in their lives, God is revealed himself through that activity and in that history. Thus, the prophetic faith proclaims not only that God speaks to our world from afar but that God enters into our world and works here. The God whom we serve is the God who has been and is with us. God is Immanuel!

6. Since God has been in the lives of people and working through their lives, the Bible also contains books which are made up primarily of humanity's response to God's revelation. The Bible contains, as we noted above, a prayer and song book. In these prayers and songs we hear people speaking to their God, but they do not speak on their own, for God was in their lives, inspiring them in their prayers and songs. It is because God was in their lives, inspiring them, that these books became part of God's revelation to us. We see this same kind of revelation in the wisdom literature of the Old Testament and in much of the instruction given to the early church in the letters of the New Testament. In these books we hear people speak to their fellow believers concerning the application and the relevance of God's primary revelation for their daily lives. For example, we heard Paul give instruction to the Corinthian church concerning marriage and then we heard him say, "I think I have the

---

5   Saifi, *Presenting Islam to the Christians*, 32.

Spirit of God." The church has always agreed with Paul. God was in the life and thinking of Paul and also with the authors of Job and Proverbs, leading these men to see how people should conduct their daily lives in the presence of God.

7. Since God has willed to be Immanuel, God with us, God speaks in and through the lives of ordinary people. For this reason the Bible is a very human book, and it is a book which reflects the ideas and feelings of those who wrote them, even though these ideas and feelings may reflect human limitation. The writers of Psalm 30 did not as yet understand the victory which God gives to God's people over death, but no one would say that God had not inspired the joyful prayer of this person! The writer of Psalm 137 had not come to understand that God wishes people to love and pray for their enemies, but no one would say that God did not inspire the writer's love for God's temple in Jerusalem. The writer of Genesis 1 did not understand the scientific view of the universe, yet no one would deny that God had inspired the writer to proclaim that God was the creator and Lord of all things. The Bible is a very human book because God has chosen to be in the world of ordinary people. The humanness of the Bible is, therefore, part of God's Good News, for it means that God has been in the lives of persons like you and me and that God can be and is in our lives. God is Immanuel!

8. Islam denies that the Qur'an is in any way a human book. Every word has come down from heaven. This means that if one can find one error in the Qur'an, the whole Islamic understanding of revelation collapses. As the Christians read the Qur'an, written in the seventh century, they believe that they find such errors, for they see that many of the biblical stories found there contradict the stories found in the Bible. For example, the New Testament plainly teaches that Jesus grew and developed as any other child (Lk 3:39, 40, 52). However, the Qur'an states that Jesus proclaimed a prophetic message in a cradle, shortly after his birth (Surah 5:110, compare 19:29). Perhaps Muhammad had heard stories of Christ from an heretical Gnostic Christian church. These Gnostic churches, for example, denied that Jesus had died on the cross. Basilides, a Gnostic writer of the second century, writes:

> Then the Unborn and Unnamed Father...sent his First begotten Mind (and this is he they call the Christ), for the freeing of them that believe in him from those who made the world. And he appeared to the nations of them as a man on the earth, and performed deeds of virtue. Wherefore he suffered not, but a certain Simon, a Cyrenian, was impressed to bear his cross for him; and

Simon was crucified in ignorance and error, having been transfigured
by him, that men should suppose him to be Jesus, while Jesus
himself took on the appearance of Simon and stood by and mocked
them.[6]

This Gnostic belief took many forms and it seems that this type of
story had been heard and believed by Muhammad. For this reason the
Qur'an says that the Jews said, "We slew the Messiah, Jesus son of Mary,
Allah's messenger." However, the Qur'an adds, "They slew him not nor
crucified, but it appeared so unto them" (Surah 4:157). The Christian
faith, on the other hand, powerfully asserts that Jesus was crucified, dead,
and buried. These two Qur'anic illustrations from the life of Jesus
contradict the biblical witness. On purely historical grounds, it would seem
that Mark, writing in about the year 66 A.D. and Luke writing a short time
later, should have more accurate information concerning the life of Jesus
than Muhammad writing 700 years later. Furthermore, several of the
Qur'anic stories about Jesus are known to be found in heretical gospels
and writings which were rejected by the early Church because they were
nonapostolic and late in date. The Qur'anic version of the crucifixion
would be one example. Another would be the Qur'anic story which tells
of how the boy Jesus made mud birds and then caused them to fly, a story
which is related in the Gospel of Thomas (Surah 5:110, compare with The
Gospel of Thomas II). These stories would seem to indicate that
Muhammad accepted this false information about Jesus as true and then
these stories later became part of his message. If this is true, it means
that the Qur'an is very fallible and the Islamic view of revelation collapses
and with it the *present* Islamic view of the Qur'an.

Muslims obviously would not accept this argument, because their
faith assumes the absolute inerrancy of the Qur'an. All Christian scriptures
are subject to correction by the infallible Word of God, the Qur'an. If
Muslims ever accept the fact that the Qur'an contains mistakes, they will
no doubt alter their views concerning revelation and the Qur'an. Then the
Muslim will have to decide to choose between Islam and Christianity on
the basis of the content of the messages of the Bible and the Qur'an. The
Qur'an proclaims one way in which God acts and deals with humanity; the
Bible proclaims another. God in the form of Allah, the beneficent, the

[6]Basilides, *Documents of the Christian Church*, ed. Henry Bettenson (1943; reprint London:
Oxford University Press, 1960), 51.

merciful, calls; God in the form of the Father of our Lord Jesus Christ calls. Which form is the true image of God, the Creator and Lord of all things? To which call does the Holy Spirit lead people to answer?

APPENDIX 1 BIBLIOGRAPHY

Basilides, *Documents of the Christian Church*. Edited by Henry Betterson. 1943; reprint, London: Oxford University Press.

Forde, Daryll, ed. *African Worlds*. London: Oxford University Press, 1964.

Pickthall, Muhammad M., Translated *The Glorious Qur'an*. 1953; reprint, New York: New American Library of World Literature, 1960.

Saifi, Nasum. *Presenting Islam to the Christians*. Lagos: Chief Ahmadiyya Bookshop, 1961.

GENERAL BIBLIOGRAPHY

In addition to the volumes listed below, see bibliography in Appendix 1.

Altmann, Walter. "Interpreting the Doctrine of the Two Kingdoms." *Word and World*, Winter 1987: 54-55.

—. *Luther and Liberation: A Latin American Perspective.* Minneapolis: Fortress Press, 1992.

Ariarajah, Wesley. *The Bible and People of Other Faiths.* Geneva: World Council of Churches, 1985.

—. *Hindus and Christians: A Century of Protestant Ecumenical Thought.* Grand Rapids: Eerdmans Publishing, 1991.

Aulen, Gustav. *Christus Victor.* New York: Macmillan, 1931.

Baille, D. M. *God Was in Christ: An Essay on Incarnation and Atonement.* New York: Charles Scribner's Sons, 1955.

Barrett, David B. "Annual Statistical Table on Global Mission." *International Bulletin* 16 (January 1992): 26.

Barth, Karl. *The Doctrine of the Word of God.* Vol. 1, part 1. *Prolegomena to Church Dogmatics.* Edinburgh: T. & T. Clark, 1936.

Bijlefeld, Willem A. "Christian Witness in an Islamic Context," *God and Jesus: Theological Reflections for Christian Muslim Dialog* [1986]. Division for World Mission and Inter-Church Cooperation, The American Lutheran Church, Minneapolis, Minnesota. Photocopy. A collection of papers prepared by The American Lutheran Church's Board for World Mission and Inter-Church Cooperation Task Force on Christian Witness Among Muslims, 1984-86.

Boer, Harry. *Pentecost and Missions*. London: Lutherworth, 1961.

Boff, Leonardo and Clodovis. *Introducing Liberation Theology*. Maryknoll, New York: Orbis Books, 1987.

Boff, Leonardo. *Way of the Cross—Way of Justice*. Maryknoll, New York: Orbis Books, 1982.

Bonhoeffer, Dietrich. *Letters and Papers from Prison*. London: Collins-S.C.M. Press, 1953; enl. ed. New York: Macmillan Publishing, 1971.

Borg, Marcus J. *Jesus: A New Vision*. Harper & Row, 1987.

Braaten, Carl. *The Apostolic Imperative*. Minneapolis: Augsburg Publishing, 1985.

—. *The Flaming Center: A Theology of Christian Mission*. Philadelphia: Fortress Press, 1977.

—. *No Other Gospel: Christianity Among the World's Religions*. Minneapolis: Fortress Press, 1992.

Brunner, Emil. *The Word and the World*. London: S.C.M. Press, 1931.

Buddhadasa Bhikkhu. *Buddha-Dhamma for Students*. Translated by Ariyananda Bhikkhu (Roderick S. Bucknell). Rev. Ed. Chiang Mai, Thailand: Buddha-Nigama Association, 1972; reprint. Bangkok: Dhamma Study and Practice Group with help from Evolution/Liberation, 1988.

Butterfield, Herbert. *Christianity and History*. New York: Charles Scribner's Sons, 1949.

Castro, Emilio. *Freedom in Mission: The Perspective of the Kingdom of God*. Geneva: World Council of Churches, 1985.

Cobb, John B., Jr. *Beyond Dialog: Toward a Mutual Transformation of Christianity and Buddhism*. Philadelphia: Fortress Press, 1982.

Cragg, Kenneth. *The Call of the Minaret*. Rev. ed. Maryknoll, New York: Orbis, 1989.

—. *The Christ and the Faiths*. Philadelphia: Westminster Press, 1986.

—. *Muhammad and the Christian: A Question of Response*. Maryknoll, New York: Orbis, 1984.

Crossan, John Dominic. *The Historical Jesus: The Life of a Mediterranean Jewish Peasant*. San Francisco: HarperCollins, 1991.

Deane, S. N., trans. *Saint Anselm. Basic Writings: Proslogium, Monologium, and Appendix*. 1962. 2nd ed. Reprint. LaSalle, Illinois: Open Court Publishing, 1966.

Denny, Frederick Mathewson. *An Introduction to Islam*. New York: Macmillian Publishing, 1985.

Fiorenza, Elisabeth Schüssler. *In Memory of Her: A Feminist Theological Reconstruction of Christian Origins*. New York: Crossroad, 1984.

Forde, Gerhard. "Eleventh Locus, Christian Life, Justification Today." *Christian Dogmatics*. Vol. 2. Edited by Carl Braaten and Robert Jenson. Philadelphia: Fortress Press, 1984.

Forell, George. *History of Christian Ethics*. Vol 1. Minneapolis: Augsburg Publishing, 1979.

—. *The Protestant Faith*. Englewood Cliffs: Prentis-Hall, 1960.

Fretheim, Terence E. "God and Prophet: An Old Testament Perspective," *God and Jesus: Theological Reflections for Christian-Muslim Dialog*. [1986]. Division for World Mission and Inter-Church Cooperation, The American Lutheran Church, Minneapolis, Minnesota. Photocopy. A collection of papers prepared by The American Lutheran Church's Board for World Mission and Inter-Church Cooperation Task Force on Christian Witness Among Muslims, 1984-86.

—. *The Suffering of God: An Old Testament Perspective*. Philadelphia: Fortress Press, 1984.

Gandhi, M. K. *What Jesus Means to Me*. Compiled by R. K. Prabhu. Ahmedabad: Navajivan Publishing, 1959.

Gibb, H. A. R. *Mohammedanism: An Historical Survey.* 1949. 2nd ed. Reprinted with revisions. New York: Oxford University Press, 1962.

Gutierrez, Gustavo. *A Theology of Liberation: History, Politics and Salvation.* Maryknoll, New York: Orbis Books, 1973.

Hall, Douglas John. *God and Human Suffering: An Exercise in the Theology of the Cross.* Minneapolis: Augsburg Publishing, 1986.

Hauerwas, Stanley and Willimon, William H. *Resident Aliens.* Nashville: Abingdon, 1989.

Hick, John. "Whatever Path Men Choose is Mine." *Christianity and Other Religions: Selected Readings.* Edited by John Hick and Brian Hebblethwaite. Philadelphia: Fortress Press, 1981.

Jenson, Robert W. *The Triune Identity.* Philadelphia: Fortress Press, 1982.

"Justification and Justice." *Word and World,* Winter 1987: 3-98.

Kierkegaard, Søren. *Training in Christianity.* Translated with introductory notes by Walter Lowrie. London: Oxford University Press, 1941.

Kitamori, Kazo. *The Theology of the Pain of God.* Richmond: John Knox Press, 1965.

Knitter, Paul F. *No Other Name: A Critical Survey of Christian Attitude Toward the World Religions.* Maryknoll, New York: Orbis, 1985.

Koyama, Kosuke. *Waterbuffalo Theology.* Maryknoll, New York: Orbis, 1974.

Lull, Timothy F., ed. *Martin Luther's Basic Theological Writings.* Minneapolis: Fortress Press, 1989.

Luther, Martin. *Martin Luther's Basic Theological Writings.* Edited by Timothy F. Lull. Minneapolis: Fortress Press, 1989.

Martinson, Paul Varo. *A Theology of World Religions.* Minneapolis: Augsburg Publishing, 1987.

—. "Do Our Pathways Cross?" *In Suffering and Redemption: Exploring Christian Witness Within a Buddhist Context* [1988]. Division for Global Mission, Evangelical Lutheran Church in America, Chicago, Illinois. Photocopy. A collection of papers prepared by The American Lutheran Church's Board for World Mission and Inter-Church Cooperation Task Force on Christian Witness Among Buddhists, 1986-1988.

Mollenkott, Virginia Ramey. *The Divine Feminine: The Biblical Imagery of God as Female*. New York: Crossroad, 1989.

Moltmann, Jürgen. *The Crucified God: The Cross of Christ as the Foundation and Criticism of Christian Theology*. New York: Harper and Row, 1974.

Newbigin, Lesslie. *Trinitarian Faith and Today's Mission*. Richmond: John Knox Press, 1963.

Niebuhr, Reinhold. *The Nature and Destiny of Man: A Christian Interpretation*. Vol. 1. New York: Charles Scribner's Sons, 1955.

Nygren, Anders. *The Essence of Christianity*. Philadelphia: Muhlenberg Press, 1961.

Pannenberg, Wolfhart. *Jesus—God and Man*. Translated by Lewis L. Wilkens and Duane A. Priebe. Philadelphia: Westminister Press, 1968.

Rahbar, Daud. *God of Justice: A Study in Ethical Doctrine of the Qur'an*. Leiden, Netherlands: E. J. Brill, 1960.

—. "Memories and Meanings Boston" [1985]. Boston University. Photocopy.

Rahman, Fazlur. *Major Themes of the Qur'an*. Minneapolis: Bibliotheca Islamica, 1989.

Rahula, Walpola Sri. *What the Buddha Taught*. New York: Grove Press, 1974.

Saint Anselm. Basic Writings, Proslogium, Monologium, and Appendix. Translated by S. N. Deane. 2nd ed. 1962. Reprint. LaSalle, Illinois: Open Court Publishing, 1966.

Song, Choan-Seng. *Third Eye Theology: Theology in Formation in Asian Settings*. Rev. ed. Maryknoll, New York: Orbis Books, 1979.

Suzuki, Daisetz Teitaro. *An Introduction to Zen Buddhism*. New York: Grove Press, 1964.

Tappert, Theodore G., trans. and ed. *The Book of Concord: The Confessions of the Evangelical Lutheran Church*. Philadelphia: Fortress Press, 1959.

Thomsen, Mark. "A Christology of the Spirit." *Dialog* 16 (Spring 1977): 135-138.

—. "The Lordship of Jesus and Theological Pluralism." *Dialog* 9 (1972): 125ff.

Tillich, Paul. "Existence and the Christ." *Systematic Theology*. Vol. 2. Chicago: University of Chicago Press, 1957.

—. *Systematic Theology*. Vol. 3. Chicago: University of Chicago Press, 1963.

Tutu, Desmond. "The Theology of Liberation in Africa." *African Theology en Route, Papers from the Pan-African Conference of Third World Theologians, December 17-23, 1977, Accra, Ghana*. Edited by Kofi Appiah-Kubi and Sergio Torres. Maryknoll, New York: Orbis Books, 1979.

von Loewenich, Walther. *Luther's Theology of the Cross*. Minneapolis: Augsburg Publishing, 1976.

Watt, W. Montgomery. *Muhammad: Prophet and Statesman*. Oxford: Oxford University Press, 1961.

Yoder, John H. *The Politics of Jesus: Vicit Agnus Noster*. Grand Rapids: Eerdmans Publishing, 1972.